HOPE

THE RELEASE FROM BONDAGE

STELLA

LifeRich Publishing is a registered trademark of The Reader's Digest Association, Inc.

LifeRich Publishing books may be ordered through booksellers or by contacting:

LifeRich Publishing
1663 Liberty Drive
Bloomington, IN 47403
www.liferichpublishing.com
844-686-9607

ISBN: 978-1-4897-5012-9 (sc)
ISBN: 978-1-4897-5011-2 (hc)
ISBN: 978-1-4897-5013-6 (e)

Library of Congress Control Number: 2024901793

Print information available on the last page.

LifeRich Publishing rev. date: 04/09/2024

DEDICATION

This book is dedicated to every soul who has hurt so deeply you
were not convinced you would make it. You have been thrown
under the bus and left for someone else's new adventure. You have
lost "you" somewhere along the way and struggled to regain your
identity. Maybe it was who you were when you were 15 or 25, before
a destructive marriage or the loss of someone precious. Please know,
I've been there…not knowing who to trust or where to turn.
My prayer as you read these pages, is that you seek and
develop the MOST intimate relationship with Jesus Christ.
That you bear your broken spirit to Him and allow Him to
take you through the time and space required to heal.
My hope is for you to be WHOLE…in Him. May He be your
center of gravity with which everything else must fall in place.
The situations and storytelling in this devotional are REAL, but the
names have been changed to protect those I hold so dear. To the ones
I have unknowingly and unwantedly hurt in the past because I was
so hurt and wounded myself. By God's grace, they too will be okay.

INTRODUCTION

Hey…we will start with a typical greeting from the South. My name is Stella. We are about to embark on a journey together. The names have been changed to protect the not so innocent. I believe it only fair to inform you I have been an emergency department Registered Nurse for several decades. I have seen and heard much, even said and done much. The ditties from my years of dealing with the "real world" will be interjected to lighten the load and bring clarity and provide a human reality to the story. I am a very REAL kinda girl, and this book is for REAL.

As you peruse each page, reread a portion that is of particular significance in your own life. My hope is you will gain new insight into the character of Jesus Christ our Lord…who He really is and who He can be in your life. My desire is to assist you with recognizing Him in the crevices of what can become the mundane of every day.

Jesus does not necessarily fall into the mold you mentally concocted while sitting in a church pew listening to the pastor radiate Biblical truths. I want you to KNOW Him, not just head knowledge of our Savior. By the end of this literary composition, may you know…that you know…that you truly KNOW Jesus as Lord and Savior, Friend and Redeemer, Sustainer and Provider, the same yesterday, today and tomorrow and for all of eternity.

> John 3: 14-17 (NKJV)
> And as Moses lifted up the serpent in the wilderness, even so must the Son of Man be lifted up, that whoever believes in Him should not perish but have eternal life. For God so loved the world that He gave His only begotten Son, that whoever believes in Him should not perish but have everlasting life.

For God did not send His Son into the world to condemn the world, but that the world through Him might be saved.

1 John 1: 8-9 (NKJV)
If we say that we have no sin, we deceive ourselves, and the Truth is not in us. If we confess our sins He is faithful and just to forgive us our sins and to cleanse us from all unrighteousness.

Romans 10: 9-10 (NKJV)
...that is you confess with your mouth the Lord Jesus and believe in your Heart that God has raised Him from the dead, you will be saved. For with the heart one believes unto righteousness, and with the mouth confession is made unto salvation.

If you do not know Jesus as Savior, I invite you to open your heart to Him. He loves you beyond your human finite comprehension. He gave His ALL for you, Dear One. He gave His life so you could be eternally released from the bondage of sin. You are encouraged to speak with a pastor, priest or Christian friend for more information.

We will continue plodding forward assuming you know Christ as your personal Savior.

This book is about BONDAGE and our release from it. To best understand the release, we must first examine a common definition of bondage. I want everyone to be on the same page.

BONDAGE

1. Involuntary servitude, to be enslaved
2. State of being bound by or subjected to some external power or control
3. States of being oppressed; in captivity; restraint; confinement

4. Anything that takes our focus away from serving or worshipping the Lord freely

I am aware there are many forms of bondage. God has made it clear to me that demon possession (which is very real) is not to be dealt with here. Your perception of the intended meaning is vital to the path ahead.

Bondage will be viewed through personal experiences. Much focus will be placed on relationships. After all, our purpose here on Earth is to communicate and serve one another; to be in relationship with God and one another. We will also examine time and service. Each one of these entities can be used by God for our fulfillment in the human form and to bring glory to His Name.

Through sharing bits and pieces of my own walk, many containing sadness, emotional trauma, heartache, disappointment and other "uglies", we will uncover the reality of God in Romans 8:28. This passage of Scripture reads "and we know that all things work together for good to those who love God, to those who are the called according to His purpose. May this journey illustrate the passage from bondage to freedom…to life abundantly through tryusting in Jesus Christ.

Tryusting is a word I fabricated some years ago which means I'm trying my very best every day to trust God with all that I've got…all my heart, all my mind and all my soul. Do I fail Him? Absolutely…but God is FAITHFUL.

Unfortunately, some religious practices metaphorically live out bondage as the power of physical corruption against the freedom of life. It is the power of fear over and against the confidence of Christian faith, where ceremonial and institutional salvation must be scrupulously and painfully observed. We are on a quest to seek FREEDOM as the sons of God, emancipated by faith in Jesus Christ. My intent is to portray as accurately as possible the difficulties and chaos which accompany bondage, then demonstrate the path God revealed to me which led to freedom. Wholeness is freedom in the flesh…say "ahhh" …just let that word wash over you. Freedom…it is a refreshing salve for the soul….AHHHHHHH.

ACKNOWLEDGEMENT

In 2012, I took my three younger children to Florida to visit my oldest daughter. We were so tired on arrival that we took a nap while waiting for Amy to finish work. I fell asleep SO hard, like a coma; when I woke that afternoon, I realized God had given me a vision for a book. He gave me a clear vision of the cover and the theme. I was to capture in words my escape from bondage—my journey out of an abusive marriage.

The book was to focus on hope through Jesus Christ and serve as encouragement for others. Lord knows, I needed tons of encouragement along my path. Victor Conner, one of my fellow guardsmen, was one of the friends who walked beside me through and post-divorce. HE listened, he encouraged, he exhorted and always displayed God's grace toward me as his sister in Christ. He drove me to capture the passion of the pain I experienced.

In 2022, God sent me away from family and friends to have "free" brain time and write. After writing, working, and spending a few months alone in northern North Dakota, Victor and I spoke via phone. He asked how the writing was progressing and asked if he could edit my book.

Victor knew the back story and knew what I was trying to say. He was able to ask me to expound or clarify if my prose was not easily understood by the reader. Victor has been patient with me, kind, and a thoroughly observant editor. I could not have completed this book without him.

Thank you always, my brother in Christ,

INTERCESSORY PRAYER
When I don't know how to pray

Have you been overwhelmed lately?
Have you struggled to be thankful to God because life is kicking you over and over and over?
Can you get your thoughts together enough to pray?

Heavenly Father,

I am bowing before Your throne of GRACE, knowing I need to pray… yet, so overwhelmed by ALL that is swirling around in my head and heart…I'm struggling to find ANY words. Thank You Abba, for knowing I would have times like this. You knew I would be inadequate and be incapable of speaking coherently. In Your infinite wisdom, You equipped the Holy Spirit to groan for me (Romans 8: 26-27). AND, You gave Jesus compassion toward me so He would petition You…when I can't pray for myself (Romans 8: 34, 1 John 2: 1 and Hebrews 7: 25). Father, You are SO good and thoughtful. You understand how frail I am and how much I need You. Thank You for making a way when I see no way. Thank You, Jesus and the Holy Spirit are willing and able to make intercession for me. Bless me, I need Your PRESENCE and Your GRACE. In the Name of Jesus…Amen.

> Romans 8: 26-27 (NKJV)
> Likewise the Spirit also helps in our weaknesses. For we do not know what we should pray for as we ought, but the Spirit Himself makes intercession for us with groanings which cannot be uttered. Now He who searches the hearts

knows what the mind of the Spirit is, because He makes intercession for the saints according to the will of God.

Romans 8: 34 (ESV)
Who is to condemn? Christ Jesus is the one who died—more than that, who was raised—who is at the right hand of God, who indeed is interceding for us.

1 John 2: 1 (NKJV)
My Little children, these things I write to you, so that you may not sin. And if anyone sins, we have an Advocate with the Father, Jesus Christ the righteous.

Hebrews 7:25 (ESV)
Consequently, He is able to save to the uttermost those who draw near to God through Him, since He always lives to make intercession for them.

HOW CAN I TRUST GOD?

How can I trust God when I do not know HIS will or see HIS plan? Faith is believing what you cannot see and trusting what has not yet happened.

In John 20 (NKJV), Now Thomas, called the twin, one of the twelve, was not with them when Jesus came. The other disciples therefore said to him, "we have seen the Lord."

So he said to them, "unless I see in HIS hands the print of the nails, and put my finger into the print of the nails, and put my hand into HIS side, I will not believe."

And after eight days HIS disciples were again inside, and Thomas with them. Jesus came, the doors being shut, and stood in the midst, and said, "Peace to you!" Then HE said to Thomas, "Reach your finger here, and look at MY hands; and reach your hand here and put it into My side. Do not be unbelieving but believing.

If one of the disciples, who walked with Jesus and witnessed the miracles HE performed had doubts, why would we be doubt-free? Doubting is one of Satan's weapons to interfere with our growth as believers.

Hebrews 11 (NASB1995)

Now FAITH is the assurance of things hoped for, the conviction of things not seen. For by it the people of old received their commendation. By faith we understand that the universe was created by the word of God, so that what is seen was not made out of things that are visible.

By faith Abel offered to God a more acceptable sacrifice than Cain, through which he was commended as righteous, God commending him by accepting his gifts. And through his faith, though he died, he still speaks. By faith Enoch was taken up so that he should not see death, and he was not found, because God had taken him. Now before he was taken he was commended as having pleased God. And without faith it is impossible to please him, for whoever would draw near to God must believe that he exists and that he rewards those who seek him. By faith Noah, being warned by God concerning events as yet unseen, in reverent fear constructed an ark for the saving of his household. By this he condemned the world and became an heir of the righteousness that comes by faith.

If you continue to read Hebrews 11, you will see one account after another of Biblical figures who believed what God told them although their eyes had not yet seen. Think about how you would feel if you read a verse "by FAITH, your name, believed God for … and it was counted to him/her as righteousness". That is better than winning the lottery.

One thing I have learned along my faith walk is that I can TRUST the character of God. When I cannot see the steps of the path ahead and I am trying to understand God's instructions, I can be assured that His instructions will NEVER violate HIS character or His WORD.

I am thankful to say I have heard the voice of God. Whether HE reveals HIMSELF to me in Scripture, in a dream, or a still small voice. I have heard HIM and HIS instructions. The key to hearing from God is to stay close to HIM. Regular Bible study, prayer time and speaking with other believers are all ways of keeping close to the Father. When you feel that God is far away, HE is not the one who moved. You are. You have strayed, fallen away or gotten too busy. Great news is, God is omnipresent—HE is right there. All you must do is acknowledge HIM. HE will gleefully welcome you back to HIM. It can be as simple as saying "help" or tears streaming down your face in brokenness. God is full of compassion and will hear your cry.

When Jesus was preparing to leave the disciples, HE knew they were anxious about functioning without HIM. It was at that time Jesus informed the disciples the Comforter (the Helper) would come once HE departed the Earth. God the Father saw their need and would provide a Guide, the Holy Spirit. We are most fortunate in modern times to have the Holy Spirit to comfort, guide and exhort us. When our faith is challenged, the Holy Spirit will remind us of God's goodness, how HE sustains and provides, how HE comforts, and makes a way when we see no way.

Have faith my friend. God desires our TRUST. Even if it is imperfect "TRYUSTING" as mentioned in the introduction. Keep "TRYUSTING"… You will fail, you will fall, but God will not.

CATTAILS #1

God brought this Southern girl to northern North Dakota in January of a very snowy year. My friends thought I was nuts and the locals could not understand me due to the Southern accent I had cultivated by living in the South my entire life.

Arriving when the temperatures were mainly below zero, I was so enraptured by the Cattails—brown and dry looking stalks that stood strong and proud through several inches of ice and snow. Have you had a time when God gave you the strength to stand when all the forces around should have broken you and made you shrivel?

I began to study the exceptional characteristics of cattails. What I discovered is, wherever there are cattails…there is a water source. You may not be able to see the water source, but it does not negate the fact the water source is nearby, providing life-sustaining nutrients.

Where there is water, there is life. Are you in survival mode? Have you been trudging through difficult circumstances? You need a long quenching drink that satisfies your soul. When Jesus spoke with the Samaritan woman at the well, he knew her history and observed her need. She had a spiritual need that He could fill. Jesus spoke of the "Living Water" of salvation. She needed a Savior and the ongoing relationship that follows.

Once Jesus left this Earth, the Holy Spirit was sent to dwell inside EACH believer. The Spirit is Comforter and Guide as we make our way along our journey. As Christians, we are connected to and receiving nourishment from the Spring of Living Water…our salvation. Drink from the well regularly, for as humans we become easily depleted and discouraged.

Thank You Jesus for thinking of our needs. Thank You for loving us enough to welcome us with open arms each and every time we hit a speed bump or make an unwise decision. 1 John 1:9 (NKJV) tells us "if we confess our sins, He is faithful and just to forgive us our sins and to cleanse us from ALL unrighteousness."

Spend time with Jesus. Drink from the well.

CATTAILS #2

Are you wounded? Do you feel bruised or tattered from what life has thrown your way? The cattails appear as a "bruised reed". Isaiah 42 (NKJV) shows us "A bruised reed HE will not break, and smoking flax HE will not quench; HE will bring forth justice for truth. HE will not fail nor be discouraged, till HE has established justice in the Earth."

The English word bruise is weak compared to the Hebrew meaning of "crushed". A bruise indicates a superficial injury that will most likely heal without struggle. Crushed implies an internal, deep wound with the potential to injure vital organs. This type of injury can leave lasting effects long after the wrongdoing has passed. Is the reed in Isaiah bruised in a manner to where it will never produce grain? Examine the cattails, how the incessant winter wind chips away the exterior and mars the integrity of the plant. Yet the cattail, with its roots securely seated in the life-sustaining water withstands the subzero temperatures and high velocity winds that sweep the Great Plains of North Dakota. When the time is right, the ice melts and the cattails release their seeds then produce again. While we may be outwardly tattered or torn by life's challenges and attacks, a soul which has been bathed and soothed by our Heavenly Father can withstand the wields of Satan with his ceaseless attacks. Have you been crushed by circumstances?

I do not wish to make light of anyone's suffering. Some wounds go deep and the pain remains for a long period of time. A long-time friend may choose to stop speaking with you and that hurts. Depending on the extent of the friendship will determine how significant the pain. However painful this may be, I hope we can agree this would be an example of a bruise in most cases. In comparison, finding out your spouse has been having an affair with someone you considered a Friend would be more along the lines of crushed. The spouse you love and have vowed to spend your life with has chosen to be intimate with another. Worse than your discovery, your spouse has no remorse regarding the infidelity and displays no compassion toward your brokenness. Crushed is an appropriate descriptive word to use because your entire life has been torn apart and seemingly shattered. I pray if you find yourself crushed, you can identify with confidence that "Jesus is with me" in these moments of sheer terror and pain. Your heart may race, and you may feel you will not be able to breathe, and you may cease living because the shock and burden of truth is so overwhelming and difficult to bear. This is "crushed" my friend. When you feel your chest caving in and you gasp to take your nest breath, I hope you can feel Jesus in your presence. Your reality is that the pain is too much to bear and you are not convinced you will survive this space and time. Remember Jesus is always with you in the darkness of your pain.

Do you feel you are too broken to be of use in God's Kingdom? Look at the life of David—he committed murder, committed adultery, and slayed thousands of individuals in battle. God used David time and time again. David is the ONLY person who ever lived, that God claims is "a man after My own heart". David suffered from anxiety and depression. What David did correctly was—he consistently ran to God with ALL his emotions and tribulations. David also gave God the victory!!!

Surrender to HIM, lay your burdens at God's throne of MERCY and COMPASSION. HE will heal you, mold you and shape you...and use you for HIS GLORY and to further the Kingdom. Praise HIM! If you are harboring unforgiveness—lay it down and don't pick it up again. Are you suffering from unconfessed sin? Confess it. Ask God to search your heart for any impurities that might be holding you back. Trust HIS evaluation of your heart. Jeremiah 17: 9-10 KJV reads "the heart is deceitful above all things, and desperately wicked; who can know it? I the Lord search the heart, I try the reins, even to give every man according to his ways, and according to the fruit of his doings."

When you are crushed, run to the Healer. Run to HIM over and over and over again, for HE never grows weary spending time with HIS broken children. In due season, you will blossom and flourish. God is merciful. HE only peels off the scabs of the wounds you can face at that time. If you get frustrated because your healing process drags on, remember it IS a process and it is on God's timeline.

AH LORD GOD, THANK YOU FOR THE MESSENGERS!!

For Your word's sake, and according to Your own heart,
You have done all these great things, to make Your
servant know them. You are great, O Lord God. For
there is none like You, nor is there any God besides You,
according to all that we have heard with our ears.
2 Samuel 7: 21 & 22 (NKJV)

My oldest daughter, Amy was called at age 10 to foster and adopt children. This was well known in our family and circle of friends. To my surprise, Amy did give birth to a biological daughter, Grace. With her ongoing passion for taking in children which she did not conceive and bear, I was not convinced Amy would have any biological offspring.

Amy and her husband muddled through having a foster child here and a foster child there, each for short periods of time. The week before the world shut down in 2020, Amy and hubby received the call Amy had yearned for. In the next 3 hours, her home would be blessed with 2 babies (5-month-old girl and her 17-month-old brother) who had to be emergently removed from a violent situation on a Friday night. Amy was gleefully shopping at Wal-Mart for diapers and butt cream while her hubby was at home assembling the port-a-crib. The joy I heard in Amy's voice that night was no less than a sugar hungry child who had been given the keys to the candy shop and no boundaries.

D and K stole Amy's heart and quickly became siblings for Grace. As the months went by, D and K made great strides to heal from the traumatic events prior to arriving at Amy's home. Our family has numerous adopted members, so we too freely embraced "the babies" and considered them family. Our love for them grew.

During the Summer of 2021, decisions were evident in the court system that "the babies" would soon be reunited with the bio mom and/ or dad before the end of the year. We were devastated. God knew how undone we were as a family, especially Amy.

I have two long-term friends, Matt and Cecilia, who I called to prayer warrior status. I petitioned each of them to pray for this situation of "the babies" leaving Amy's home. Matt and Cecilia know me, but do not know one another. Matt confidently informed me "God is protecting the children; you must claim this miracle and the miracle will happen. You must claim the miracle first." Around the same time, I was fortunate to have lunch with Cecilia and relay to her my concerns about "the babies". I told her nothing about what Matt said. Cecilia proclaimed emphatically, "God is protecting the children. You must thank Him for the miracle and the miracle will come."

Holy cow, how can I thank God for the miracle when I don't see anything but my daughter's heart collapsing and "the babies" potentially being placed in harm's way? My emotions were not wrapped around praising God. I really had to pray. God had work to do in my heart. I cried and prayed, prayed and cried, tried my best to be of support to Amy during those months. I told her we must trust the messengers. God has sent the messengers for reassurance; we must trust although we cannot see Him at work. This was a test of our faith, believing what we cannot see.

The military had placed me in Gulfport, MS the Summer of 2021. As I drove down to the beach, I felt a pull toward St. John, the Evangelist Catholic Church near the shore. Growing up Protestant, this pull toward the Catholic Church felt unusual yet strong. I had visited Amy and "the babies" a few times in a couple of months, each time we dreaded the days ahead when "the babies" would have to leave. One week was particularly difficult, many tears and tossing at night asking God "why"? "Why do the babies have to leave?"

I woke up Sunday morning, catapulted out of bed knowing I had to attend church at St. John's that morning. No other plan was right. I made my way to the church and sat in the back row. Within five minutes of entering the church, the priest began to pray. He thanked God for protecting the children. My jaw dropped, God had brought me to this service. We sang a few songs, and the priest began to deliver the sermon. It was about Jesus feeding the 5000. The priest told of how Jesus took the meager human donation of five loaves and two fish, went before the Father and gave thanks before the miracle happened. Jesus thanked God and God provided enough to feed the 5000 men, in addition to women and children, with ample supply left over.

As you can imagine, at this point the tears were streaming down my face. God brought me to this service so I could hear His promise one more time. It was the reassurance I needed as grandmother to these precious babies. When God pushes you out of your comfort zone, you can grow. While I was raised Protestant, I know in Heaven, there will be no denominations. There will be individuals of all color, race, national origin and denomination praising one Lord and Savior, Jesus Christ. Ah Lord God, thank You for the messengers. May we be ever aware and willing to listen. Calm us, as we trust You to protect the children.

THE SAUDADE

I know what you are thinking…what on Earth is she talking about? Somehow, I started receiving daily emails with a new vocabulary word. Being the nerd that I am, I was intrigued and regularly embraced the opportunity to enhance my command of the English language. Saudade is a noun that emerges from Portuguese folk lore meaning a deep emotional state of melancholic longing for a person or thing that is absent. Aha…now you are with me. Going forward you have a word to describe the feeling you have had and just did not know what to call it.

Beginning at age 11, I had the overwhelming desire to have six children. Yes, I attempted lying supine, but the feeling never went away. Then I was informed by a physician at age 18 I would have difficulty conceiving, but God had other plans.

Andy and I married in the Fall of 1987 with the continuing debate of him wanting two children, no more… me on the other hand wanting six children, no less. After birthing Amy, and two years later Jake, I was consoled by the fact God had blessed me with one of each. I vividly remember riding home from the hospital that bleak and chilly Christmas morning feeling quite blessed. Jake was born December 23rd, so we were about the only ones traveling the highways. If it was not in God's plan for me to have more children, I had the privilege of being mom to a daughter and a son. I was basking in this revelation of God's goodness.

Conceiving children seemed to be one of mine and Andy's talents. We did not have too many marriage successes, but we could breed, and boy did we. Several times we thought I was pregnant and knew his mother would have a conniption fit if this was true. We made plans to avoid his parents for months or years if necessary to avoid any arguments with them. Like they wouldn't find out??? Young and dumb.

So here is the lineup, Amy was born in early 1990, Jake the end of 1991, Tuck in 1995, Olivia in 1998 and Elisabeth in 2000.

I had a miscarriage between Tuck and Olivia and another after Lizzy. Go ahead…I know you are counting. Yes, at this point we had seven pregnancies and five children. But someone was missing…saudade. For me, there was someone who had not yet arrived. This longing for the missing one was consuming. Where could this child be? Was it one I had miscarried? Was I not seeing life correctly? Was I just totally crazy? Anyone would have to be at least half crazy to desire six kids, right?

I have always been a night owl, so it was not uncommon for me to be awake after EVERYONE in my home was sound asleep. One night, I was overcome, distraught having an overwhelming need to pray…a compulsion. I started with Amy. I went to her bedside and knelt so humbly before God. I prayed everything I could possibly think of to pray on her behalf…tears streaming down my face. One by one, I painstakingly went to each child's bed, oldest to youngest and repeated my specific petitions for each precious one. At that time, our home was three stories so I tiptoed throughout the house until I got to Lizzy in the crib. The tears were blinding by this point.

This is where TRUST comes in. I sobbed next to her crib. Father, You and You alone can make me whole. I have always thought there were six. You have blessed me far beyond anything I deserve by giving me five beautiful healthy children. There are many women who are not able to have ONE. Father, if there is not a #6, PLEASE make me whole…take the desire away…help me feel complete. God, You can do this if there is not another child for me.

There, on the floor of my youngest daughter's room, next to her crib with her resting like a cherub…I SURRENDERED. I released any amount of control I thought I had. I was trusting God to either provide the child I thought would come, or that He…God Almighty would quench my desire. I was trusting Him with the decision…the outcome…it was His choice. Little did I know that night, I was three weeks pregnant with child #6. God knew, but it was too early for me to have any symptoms. He wanted my heart; He was already sending the child.

As little Gabe grew inside of me, I could confidently announce to others that God had promised me this child. He was honoring my trust and surrender to His Sovereignty. After Gabe was born, he had trouble gaining weight. I had to cling to what I knew God had promised. He had promised this child. Many prayed for this little fellow to gain weight, and he did. I knew, that I knew, that I knew Gabe would be okay because God is FAITHFUL.

Remember the waiting? I had the desire for six children since age 11. Gabe was born when I was 39. It took 28 years for God to give me the desires of my heart. I learned so much more about Him in the waiting.

Psalm 37: 3-7 (NKJV)

Trust in the Lord, and do good, dwell in the land, and feed on His faithfulness. Delight yourself also in the Lord, and He shall give you the desires of your heart. Commit your way to the Lord, trust also in Him, and He shall bring it to pass. He shall bring forth your righteousness as the light, and your justice as the noonday. Rest in the Lord and wait patiently for Him.

WHEN YOUR ENTIRE WORLD IS CAVING IN #1

What has knocked you down? Can you recover? I will discuss a few real-life circumstances, either I have endured or someone near and dear to me has endured, by the GRACE of God.

Scenario #1: You are a beautiful young lady, methodically and diligently pursuing your education to be the best in your field. You are attending training seminars, adding skills to your toolbox, and caring for those in your community. You are married to "the love of your life", so you thought on your wedding day. He appears to be a family man, stays close to home, does not mind being involved in the housework and loves to cook. He does not cause waves with your family and provides a decent wage.

You and your husband have fun together, have mutual friends, attend family get togethers and act like a normal couple. There does not appear to be any problems regarding your intimacy in the bedroom.

As the years of your marriage unfold, you become acutely aware that your husband is emotionally detached. And on further examination, you start to unravel the fact he may have never had an emotional connection with you. Looking even more deeply, is he connected to anyone? Your gut is telling you something is not right. He seems okay in the bedroom, but something is not right. You get suspicious and start to investigate. You check his phone and there are numerous exchanges with a certain someone. Not just someone, but one you consider a friend and one who is deeply connected to your family. What is going on?

Then THE night comes, you have scrounged around and found enough courage and evidence to confront your husband about the affair. All at once, the life you have been trying to create with him turns into a complete LIE and the walls are crashing in around you. How could he? And how could he with this person? Not only has he destroyed any fiber of marriage integrity, but he has absolutely and totally violated your family.

The thoughts are racing, your heart is racing. Do you cry, do you scream in rage, and worse - "she" is currently visiting in your home!!!! Do you strike out at them both? Do you leave? If you leave, are you safe to drive? Who knows? The tears have been fulminating out of your eyes for hours. If you kick your husband out, will he run to the other woman? If you leave, where will you go? You have friends, but your entire family lives at least 300 miles away.

The confusion and chaos of this dreaded night find you in a fetal position on the bathroom floor and wishing you were dead. Your husband stands over you, possessing no compassion for your pain. It is as if he justifies his actions. Is there any escape? Where do you turn? Who do you call at midnight or 4am when your entire life has turned into a sham? You have been faithful, you have been loving, you have been giving, and it is just not enough. You wonder, am I enough? Will I ever be enough? What went wrong? And when?

You are not sure how you moved an ounce of your body from the bathroom floor, but somehow you managed to get to the closet in your bedroom. The bedroom you have shared for years with your husband. You are now crouched up in the back corner of the closet, your sweet puppy has come to give you comfort. Your back is hunched up against the wall of the closet; as tight as you can gather yourself into a ball. You are resting on an animal hair covered, needing to be washed, dog bed as you weep in anguish. This is the elevation of your life, lower than low. There is NO ONE on this Earth who is or can be with you in this moment. You are consumed by the devastating truth that your committed has had sex with another woman, and she has been so intricately woven into your life and your family for years. How do you take your next breath? How do you keep your chest from caving in? How do you get your heart rate to slow down enough to think about breathing normally?

A little while later when you hear your Mom's voice on the phone and you begin to explain the terror you have survived in the previous 6 hours, you are able to squeak out in humble confidence, "Jesus was with me". It was in the middle of processing this horrific truth in my life, I knew my daughter would be okay. Jesus was with her.

As parents we wish to protect our children, but we cannot always be in the right space at the right time. The lessons they endure are part of their spiritual growth. I am eternally thankful my dear daughter had grown in her trust of Jesus as Savior, Sustainer, and Friend; and she could recognize in her deepest, darkest, most sorrowful night that HE was with her. HE will NEVER leave us or forsake us. Jesus is FAITHFUL.

If you find yourself in a similar situation, I encourage you to cling to God's promises in His WORD:

Be strong and of good courage, do not fear nor be afraid of them; for the Lord your God, He is the One who goes with you. He will not leave you nor forsake you (Deuteronomy 31, NKJV). And again a few verses later, "the Lord, He is the One who goes before you. He will be with you, He will not leave you nor forsake you; do not fear nor be dismayed".

No temptation has overtaken you except what is common to mankind. And God is faithful; He will not let you be tempted beyond what you can bear. But when you are tempted, He will also provide a way out so that you can endure it (1 Corinthians 10:13 summarized).

Cast all your care upon Him, for He cares for you 1 Peter 5: 7 (NKJV).

Let us then approach God's throne of grace with confidence, so that we may receive MERCY and find GRACE to help us in our time of need (Hebrews 4: 16).

Marriage is honorable among all, and the bed undefiled; but fornicators and adulterers God will judge Hebrews 13: 4 (NASB).

So we say with confidence, "The Lord is my helper; I will not be afraid. What will man do to me?" Hebrews 13: 6 (ESV).

Have I not commanded you? Be strong and of good courage; do not be afraid, nor be dismayed, for the LORD your God will be with you wherever you go Joshua 1: 9 (NIV).

Do not gloat over me, my enemy! Though I have fallen, I will rise. Though I sit in darkness, the LORD will be my light Micah 7: 8 (summarized).

A portion of the Prayer of St. Patrick

Christ shield me today
Against poison, against burning,
Against drowning, against wounding,
So that reward may come to me in abundance.
Christ with me, Christ before me, Christ behind me,
Christ in me, Christ beneath me, Christ above me,
Christ on my right, Christ on my left,
Christ when I lie down, Christ when I sit down,
Christ in the heart of every man who thinks of me,
Christ in the mouth of every man who speaks of me,
Christ in the eye that sees me,
Christ in the ear that hears me.
(https://www.journeywithjesus.net)

WHY DON'T YOU BEND?

Are you resistant to surrendering your LIFE to Jesus? We hear the phrase "Lord of my Life", the real question is…is HE your Lord? Is HE your personal Savior? Do you surrender to His will and His way?

If not, what are your obstacles? Pride…perceived "loss of control"…stubbornness…insecurities…or just plain pride.

Do you recognize the FACT that you are unable to take your next breath if God Almighty does not grant it to you? Have you had an experience that forced you to come face-to-face with your own mortality? What impact did that experience have on your perspective of God and who HE is?

During my January/February weeks in northern North Dakota, I had an engine block heater installed to assist my car surviving the consistent subzero temperatures. For all the Southerners reading this, the process of heating the engine oil involves plugging your car into an electrical outlet. Now I pose a question. How many of you have tried to fold, mold or wrestle a heavy duty 50-foot extension cord into the back of your car when it is -25 with a windchill of -45 degrees? It is very stubborn, rigid and unbendable. As I wrestled day after day with the cord, I was reminded of how God must feel when we resist His molding of our lives. Oftentimes, our humanness gets in the way of what God is accomplishing in us and through us.

As I have traveled through life's difficulties, I have learned to trust the character of God when I cannot blatantly see His goodness. God is true to His character.

God cannot lie or deceive. (James 1:13 and Numbers 23:19, NKJV)
God is just. (Hebrews 6:10 and Colossians 3:25, NKJV)

God is holy (1 Samuel 2:2, 1 Peter 1:16, Leviticus 19:2, Isaiah 57:15, Revelation 4:8 NKJV to name a few)

God is faithful (Exodus 34:6, Deuteronomy 7:9-11, Lamentations 3:22-23 NKJV) and God knows what is best for us (Jeremiah 29:11 NKJV)

Spend time in the Presence of God, learn to trust His character. By making God your center of gravity, HE will reveal these truths to you. Isaiah 26:3 NKJV tells us "You [God] keep him in perfect peace whose mind is stayed on You, because he trusts in You." God is the same yesterday, today and forever. You can trust Him in ALL ways, for He is God.

GOD GIVES A NUDGE

I worked night shift as a nurse for many years. During this time, there was a male nurse named Isaac and he worked with me for nearly two decades. Isaac was Jewish by birth but was not raised going to temple regularly. He was haughty when anyone spoke of Jesus or Christianity. At dinner gatherings, Isaac would scoff if a blessing was uttered prior to the meal.

One Sunday afternoon, I was in the basement closet choosing my daughters' clothing for the following school day; when God notified me, "you are going to witness to Isaac tonight at work."

Me: "No God, You know how he is. He will scoff at me."

God: "You will tell Isaac about Me tonight at work."

Me: "Well, You know Sundays are busy...so You will have to make the conditions right...then probably knock me in the head to make me recognize the conditions are right." Why was I questioning God? Why was I wrestling with Him? Have you ever wrestled with God?

And with that interaction with God, I was off to work my 12-hour shift in the emergency department and Isaac was working.

The beginning of the night shift was the anticipated busy we considered "normal". The hours clicked by. Around 9 pm I found myself sitting at one of the nurses' stations next to Isaac in front of a computer screen. The emergency department is 55,000 square feet of real estate, so the chances of ending up next to a particular teammate were slim to none. I was in charge and made rounds throughout the entire department. I thought, was this my God appointment?

I looked at the computer and noted the census in the department was low. My heart began to pound knowing I had a God appointed assignment and I did not need to be defiant. Doubts raced through my head; how would Isaac receive what I had to say? Would he reject me? Would he reject Jesus? What words do I use to speak correctly to Isaac? Will I mess up my assignment?

I asked Isaac to accompany me down to the resuscitation room. It was at the end of the hallway and away from most of the staff. I thought our conversation could be more private. I had been Isaac's charge nurse for years and when I asked to speak with him in private, he assumed it was a counseling session. I convinced him I had something else to discuss and he followed me down the hallway.

Isaac reclined on the stretcher and did not utter a word for 30-45 minutes. I shared the gospel of Jesus Christ from John 14:6 NKJV which tells us Jesus said, "I am the WAY, the TRUTH, and the LIFE. No man comes to the Father except through me." I spoke of my care and concern for Isaac as a friend and I wanted him to know the saving grace of our Lord and Savior Jesus Christ.

To my surprise, Isaac listened. He listened intently. He did not offer one rebuking or scornful word in response. Isaac is a talkative soul, so the quietness with which he received the words lead me to believe he was really soaking it in. At the end of my delivery of the gospel, Isaac sat upright on the stretcher and proclaimed, "if I would accept Jesus as my Savior, Diana would agree to marry me". Diana had worked with us years prior, was a believer and did not wish to be unequally yoked in marriage with an unbeliever, though Isaac and Diana cared very much for one another. What I did not realize when God announced my assignment, is that God Himself had been softening Isaac's heart.

As we left the resuscitation room that evening, I invited Isaac to go to the movie, *Passion of the Christ* with me and my two oldest children. It was coming to theatres near us in a few weeks and I had heard great reviews. Isaac agreed. Stay tuned.

Proverbs 16: 3 (NKJV)
Commit your works to the Lord, and your thoughts will
be established.

John 15: 12-17 (NKJV)
"This is My commandment, that you love one another as
I have loved you. Greater love has no one than this, than

to lay down one's life for his friends. You are My friends if you do whatever I command you. No longer do I call you servants, for a servant does not know what his master is doing; but I have called you friend, for all things that I heard from My Father I have made known to you. You did not choose Me, but I chose you and appointed you that you should go and bear fruit, and that your fruit should remain, that whatever you ask the Father in My name He may give you. These things I command you, that you love one another."

Joshua 24: 15b (NKJV)
As for me and my house, we will serve the LORD.

Ephesians 3: 19 -21 (NKJV)
...to know the love of Christ which passes knowledge; that you may be filled with all the fullness of God. Now to Him who is able to do exceedingly abundantly above all that we ask or think, according to the power that works in us, to Him be glory in the church by Christ Jesus to all generations, forever and ever. Amen

GOD NUDGES AGAIN

If you have not read *God Gives a Nudge*, please do so before going forward with this reading. Isaac had agreed to attend the *Passion of the Christ* movie with me and my two teenage children. Andy and I decided the other children were too young to watch the graphic display of the Crucifixion. Andy was willing to stay with the younger ones while we watched the movie, then join us after for a nice Italian dinner at the local restaurant near the theater.

Amy and Jake were raised in church and familiar with the story of Christ's sufferings. I tried to prepare them for the compelling demonstration they would see on the screen. As the movie progressed, Isaac asked "how can your children just sit there and watch this movie?" Isaac was quite taken by the events leading up to the Crucifixion and began to cry.

By the movie's end, Isaac was overcome and unable to proceed to dinner. He was incredibly taken by the brutality of what Christ suffered and unable to speak to us. Isaac drove away in his convertible pondering the sacrifice made for our sins. God was sifting his heart in a manner no man could.

> 2 Corinthians 5: 17-21 (NKJV)
> Therefore, if anyone is in Christ, he is a new creation; old things have passed away; behold, all things have become new. Now all things are of God, who has reconciled us to Himself through Jesus Christ, and has given us the ministry of reconciliation, that is, that God was in Christ reconciling the world to Himself, not imputing their trespasses to them, and has committed to us the word of reconciliation. Now then, we are ambassadors for Christ,

as though God were pleading through us; we implore you on Christ's behalf, be reconciled to God. For He made Him who knew no sin to be sin for us, that we might become the righteousness of God in Him.

John 3: 11-21 (NKJV)
Most assuredly, I say to you, we speak what we know and testify what we have seen, and you do not receive our witness.

If I have told you earthly things and you do not believe, how will you believe if I tell you heavenly things?

No one has ascended to heaven but He who came down from heaven, that is the Son of Man who is in heaven.

And as Moses lifted up the serpent in the wilderness, even so must the Son of Man be lifted up, that whoever believes in Him should not perish but have eternal life.

For God so loved the world that He gave His only begotten Son, that whoever believes in Him should not perish but have everlasting life.

For God did not send His Son into the world to condemn the world but hat the world through Him might be saved.

He who believes in Him is not condemned; but he who does not believe is condemned already, because he has not believed in the name of the only begotten Son of God.

And this is the condemnation, that the light has come into the world, and men loved darkness rather than light, because their deeds were evil.

For everyone practicing evil hates the light and does not come to the light, lest his deeds should be exposed.

But he who does the truth comes to the light, that his deeds may be clearly seen, that they have been done in God.

Ephesians 3: 17-19 (NKJV)
That Christ may dwell in your hearts through faith; that you, being rooted and grounded in love, may be able to comprehend with all the saints what is the width and length and depth and height—to know the love of Christ which passes knowledge; that you may be filled with all the fullness of God.

Luke 2: 14 (NKJV)
Glory to God in the highest, and on earth peace, goodwill toward men!

SAUDADE PART 2

I am a hopeless romantic. I loved Andy when we were young, but as the years passed, I knew things were wrong between us. In 1994, I began to pray for the privilege of having an intimate emotionally fulfilling relationship with a man on this Earth. Very obviously this was not going to be a happening thing with my husband. I tried to see the good in Andy. One time after an argument with Andy, I felt convicted by the Bible study to write Andy a letter. I expressed 10 things I appreciated about him. That day it took me quite some time and a lot of digging around inside my head and heart to honestly slap something on the page. Imagine, after all my hard work and production of such a work of art, how disturbed and disheartened I was that Andy did not even open the letter for three days. After opening, he barely uttered a word in response. I could have clobbered him for his thoughtlessness.

We spent time together, it did not help. We went to counseling, it did not help. We went on a marriage retreat with our church, Andy did not participate in the class and wondered why I could not repeat our marriage vows to him. Seriously? After 17 years of a miserable marriage, I realized no amount of love for Andy would make up for the love he did not receive from his mother during his formative years. He was "mommy deprived". He failed to have the capacity for love. And in turn was abusive in his behavior toward me. I was blamed for everything and anything that went wrong in our lives.

I was the major breadwinner, the main caregiver to the children, tended the house and was expected to wash 50 loads of clothing per week, do the yardwork, cook meals and relax the way he wanted to relax— flipping through 40 channels in an hour when there were 800 things to be accomplished to keep our house going. We grew apart...farther and farther. I believe at this point in the writing process, I might be preaching to the choir.

I knew a special someone was a possibility. Some people do find true love and companionship, right? Am I a person God would see fit to bless with an earthly love? I certainly feel like I am capable of loving another and being in a mutually loving relationship. Will God allow it? For years I was, according to the old Scottish or Irish, a bit stravage. In other words, I was wandering aimlessly. I was stuck in a quagmire of confusion and chaos. Someone was missing...my saudade.

In August 2009, as I waited to board a plane to Utah, I was exposed to an enrapturing concept of God taking me outside my comfort zone to grow and to take me new places. As I read my Bible study and conversed with my mom by phone, I admitted I was ready to go where God would take me. I was ready to deploy with the military or serve Him anywhere He chose for me to go.

I had been in the military a little over a year and broadening my horizons, I was en route to several days of training for Air Force medical personnel near Salt Lake City, a place I had never been.

Prior to the trip, my chief nurse had made sure I registered for appropriate classes. The classes she was determined I would attend. She and I did not see eye to eye, but I consented and followed her lead. Once on the property, I met with colleagues and commenced to plod through the training days.

Day one I was to attend a class I did not wish to attend. My heart and head were in the other room for a desired certification. I am a nerd and at that point in my life, liked to acquire as many nursing related certifications as possible. LtCol Mary was convinced I needed not only attend the class, but also sit with her...on the front row so I could pay attention. At this moment, I morphed into a spoiled 5-year-old stance and demeanor. I puckered out my bottom lip, crossed my arms and stared straight ahead because I was convinced this day was going to bring nothing but aggravation and boredom.

Remember God works in mysterious ways. During class, members (all nurses and medics) would stand to ask questions and remain standing until the speaker answered the question. I did not turn around to view those posing questions because I was on the front row. I guessed their approximate location in the room. Well part way through the class, a male member stood, introducing himself as a member from a medical group in New York…blah, blah, blah.

He got my attention because my flight instructor from Reserved Commission Officer Training school was a nurse in the Air National Guard from New York. With 96 Medical Groups in the ANG nationally, there was a chance this guy knew my flight instructor.

On the next break, I went to the table where I thought the voice originated. A nice gentleman asked if he could help me and I proceeded to ask if he was from New York. He was not, but the member sitting next to him was from New York, had stepped away and would be returning imminently. I waited.

Much to my surprise, a strikingly handsome Lieutenant Colonel walked up, smiled big and said "Hi, how are you?" with his thick New York accent. I started to ask if he could possibly know my flight instructor, but class was ready to resume. As I turned to walk away, this LtCol asked if I was going to the nursing social later that day because he wanted to talk to me some more. Shrugging my shoulders at him, I acknowledged my intentions to attend the etiquette appropriate gathering and returned to my seat, not thinking much of our interaction.

A brief interjection here to inform the readers of where I am personally when all this is taking place. I am a miserably married woman of nearly 22 years, being reminded constantly by my abusive husband of how unlovely and unwanted I am…how undesirable I am to men. I had been seriously contemplating for 5 years how to get out and how to care for my children through a marriage split. Additionally, I had been facing consistent adversity at my civilian job for many months, thankful to feel I was somewhat of value in the military. Directly commissioning as a field grade officer (Major) had proven to have its own set of challenges and myriad of insecurities. I hope you have the picture of a shredded lump of mess when you think of me. FULL of insecurities in every avenue of my life. I did not know which end was up, nor was I sure I would survive long enough and endure well enough to care.

Back to the Lieutenant Colonel, that afternoon he made a bee line for me at the social. Inquiring as to this "connection" we MIGHT have. I tried to reassure him, Michael, that it was no big deal. He made several phone calls to see if someone he knew might know my instructor. We conversed over many things, and with several others. He was so nice to me. I was not accustomed to someone being so thoughtful toward me.

The next day, Michael was in my class. We did not sit close in the class but spoke between sessions and went with a group of members after class to tour the property. The event was hosted at a ski resort, but it was August. Michael and I ended up on the same lift chair to go up the mountain. Nothing inappropriate occurred, but it was a 16-minute ride that changed my life. I was kicking myself I was still married. My heart had not belonged to Andy for several years. I was not sure where my heart was, some days I wasn't even convinced I still had one. On the other hand, this guy was special. He was so kind and thoughtful. What do I do with this? I don't even know where to start processing this information. Is he a temptation of the devil or manna from heaven? I had no idea.

Michael and I were instant friends. What I realized over the next six months is I had finally met the other half of my soul. I had not known where he was for over four decades. Michael was my saudade. Michael and I spent time together at the conference, spoke and communicated afterward. Clarification, nothing inappropriate happened, I was married, and Michael is a Christian gentleman.

After three days at the training conference, Michael flew back home, and I returned to my life the following day. I had no idea of how to get from where I was to where I thought I wanted to be. But I knew beyond a shadow of a doubt if Michael and I ended up together he would care for me and love me with dignity until my dying breath.

I KNEW HIS PERSONALITY, BUT GOD KNEW HIS HEART

My son had pulled away from family, especially me after I divorced his father in 2010. He was participating in risky behaviors. My endless and repeated prayer was "Lord, draw him near to You". For years I cried out to the Lord on Tuck's behalf.

I knew, as his mother, he was passionate and driven. Tuck was not wishy-washy about anything. There wasn't much "grey" in his life. As the years went by and Tuck exhibited more and more risky behavior, I continued to petition God Almighty to draw him near. I added for God to "flip the switch" in my son. As time dragged on, we had many bouts of conflict, discontent, and discord were our way of life. I begged God to soften my son's heart and straighten his path. My simple words of "draw him near" and "flip the switch" became my daily plea.

Christmas time 2018, Tuck came for a visit at my new home. He came completely arrayed with all the arrogance a young male in his 20's can sport. You know, the kind that represents hurt and anger from unresolved grief. He carried much pain from the divorce and a mountain of unforgiveness, especially toward me.

As difficult as it was for me as Mommy, I knew I could not allow this attitude into my home. The home God provided—full of peace and healing. I desperately desired to spend quality time with Tuck. I approached him in the driveway before he could enter the house. Calmly I informed him that God had provided a place of peace for me, my friends, and family. There was no room for conflict in my home. If he could not come in peace,

I would have to ask him not to enter. My heart was shattered as the words exited my mouth.

Tuck immediately erupted, yelling "your God, your God…I've tried your God 5 times!!"

Before I could have a thought, my 5'1" figure detonated on Tuck's 5'10" frame, bending him over backwards on the hood of my car explaining in a most prejudicial manner, "Do you, in your stubborn pride, understand you cannot take your next breath unless God Almighty grants it?"

He and I went around and around as we had so many times before. A Jerry Springer episode might come to mind. The rest of the day is a blur. Once again, we both were drained in this unresolved and ongoing battle.

Fast forward 6 months

My oldest son Jake, the youth pastor at our church left early Monday morning with a van load of youth on the way to summer church camp. My youngest two were with him. Tuck went to North Georgia with his dad for the day. I, on the other hand, had much needed FREE time. Something I usually coveted from afar. I went shopping and to get a relaxing pedicure. I had my phone on the charger and my eyes closed in the massage chair.

When I returned to my phone, I had three missed calls from Tuck. I immediately called him, only to observe he was exquisitely short of breath. In a hesitant, almost breathless manner, he explained he thought he had a pneumothorax (collapsed lung). A few years prior, Tuck experienced a rib injury which left him in chronic pain. After countless hours of therapy and treatments, the one procedure which seemed to give some relief was dry needling. Tuck had been a scientific major in college and researched any procedure or treatment before he subjected himself to it. He knew a traumatic pneumothorax was a possibility. Tuck had the dry needling from this therapist numerous times without any problems.

Tuck told me about his location in North Georgia and I went into emergency nurse mode right away. I informed him to go directly to the nearest trauma center. Praise Jesus, he was only 15 minutes from a level 1 trauma center. I told him he needed to have a chest x-ray, see a physician, and receive a chest tube as soon as possible. He was not to allow the triage nurse to place him in the waiting room. I had been an emergency nurse for over 3 decades and knew my son was in danger if he did not receive the correct help immediately.

This took place during a time when I had a restraining order against my ex-husband. Once Tuck received his chest tube and was admitted to the hospital his dad left the hospital and I was on my way to stay with my son until he was discharged.

Once I arrived and got Tuck situated in his bed, I turned to make a pallet where I could sleep near him and help him in the night. As my back was toward my son, it was as if God whispered, "I flipped the switch". I knew that however bad this moment appeared, it would serve as the moment God got my son's attention and could turn his efforts and actions to the good. My prayers had been answered. My prayers of 7-8 years were being answered.

I have a habit of talking too much, but I knew I had to calculate and measure what words I uttered to my son. He had feared for his life this day and I did not want to say the wrong thing. God had me slowly turn toward Tuck and utter so softly and tenderly, "do you understand now that you cannot take your next breath unless God grants it to you?"

With eyes wide open like two fried eggs, he quickly responded, "I got it, I got it". We spent almost 3 days together, with me helping him to do everything—bathe, use the restroom, eat-everything. But when he was discharged, he refused to come home with me. He had me drop him off where he had been living with is roommate and longtime friend.

I continued to pray for God to "draw him near". I knew God had gotten Tuck's attention. Tuck was methodically attempting to sort out the meaning of having a collapsed lung and not being able to physically participate in sports, go to the gym or be the physical specimen he had been for years. Tuck was someone who had tried to decrease his stress by working out at the gym, so sitting around was not his forte.

Two weeks passed and I got a call from Tuck, he was in tears. He blubbered out, "God got my attention, I'm listening. I've been on a wrong path for a long time." It was then that I could confess to Tuck my ongoing prayer—for God to draw him near and to flip the switch. Tuck immediately retorted, "oh, HE flipped the switch, HE definitely flipped the switch". Part of what I've learned as a mom of adult children is you must weigh your comments, and timing is paramount.

This experience shifted Tuck's attention from self-reliance to depending on the Lord. Over the next few months, I watched my son grieve through physical changes as well as spiritual warfare. Learning to daily trust our Savior and look to HIM for guidance.

Fast forward to March 2020…when the world shut down

Tuck and I were healing, but still had a way to go. Two days before the world shut down due to COVID-19, Tuck called and needed to move into my home. His roommate needed space, no argument or conflict, just space. Tuck and I can now admit, we were each a bit afraid of what it would mean for us to live together after 10 years of not.

Through our fears and time spent together, God has provided more healing in our relationship than either one of us could have imagined. It's all about God's plan and about God's timing.

In 2022, I went to the far North to work. Tuck was my child who stayed at my house and kept it running in my absence. Tuck is now clean and sober, attending church regularly and owns his own business. We have had not ONE argument since he moved in. Wow, God has incredible plans and ways!!!

GOD'S LOVE

This story reminds me of God's LOVE and how we are His children. No matter how far away we roam, no matter what trouble we find ourselves in, no matter the condition of our mortal body, He loves us and wants what is best for us.

> Matthew 18: 10-14 (NKJV)
> "Take heed that you do not despise one of these little ones, for I say to you that in heaven their angels always see the face of My Father who is in heaven. For the Son of Man has come to save that which was lost.
>
> "What do you think? If a man has a hundred sheep, and one of them goes astray, does he not leave the nighty-nine and go to the mountains to seek the one that is straying? And if he should find it, assuredly, I say to you, he rejoices more over that sheep than over the ninety-nine that did not go astray. Even so it is not the will of your Father who is in heaven that one of these little ones should perish"

Some of you reading this passage have strife, either with a parent or with your child. Pray our Gracious Heavenly Father will work in the hearts of hurt loved ones and repair what is broken. God can peel away the veil that keeps your loved one from seeing clearly how much you love them. Better than that, He can reveal His love to your loved one so they may receive healing and embrace His everlasting love.

One of my lifetime friends taught preschool at our church when my children were growing up. She would tell the kids, "God is absolutely

CRAZY about you". At first when I heard her say this to my three-year-old daughter, I turned my head sideways and realized I never thought of God in this way. But I should have. You should as well.

Weeks ago, this same friend spoke with me at length and reminded me that God is CRAZY about me. I am much older than a preschool child, but needed the reminder just the same. We can get angry with God; we can tell Him how frustrated we are with Him and how we lack understanding of His plan…but His LOVE for us never ceases. He is happy when we confess our emotions to Him. Be gut level honest with your Abba Father and He will continue to demonstrate His unending love toward you.

Some readers may see the outpouring of anger, frustration or other like emotions to be disrespectful to God. It is not disrespectful, it is honest. The book of Psalms gives us David's relationship with God as well as David's humongous array of emotions. David took it ALL before the Father. God is big enough and loving enough to handle anything you are dealing with.

I encourage you to listen to the song sung by Casting Crowns or Lauren Daigle "Here's My Heart, Lord".

GOD ALLOWS TOUGH CIRCUMSTANCES

Please read *God Gives a Nudge* and *God Nudges Again*.

Isaac had a rough year and you have read of a few circumstances used to soften Isaac's heart. The year continued with several speed bumps; Isaac was a talented musician and enjoyed playing instruments with his friends. One evening he traveled to North Georgia to play music with one of our coworkers. They enjoyed a few adult beverages as the evening wore on. They continued to play music and ingest more alcohol.

The evening ended, Isaac loaded up his instruments in his convertible, and began his trek home near Atlanta. He was stopped by the police and determined to be driving under the influence. Isaac was taken to the nearby jail in a small not quickly changing town in the North Georgia mountains. Remember Isaac was Jewish by birth; so, he had experienced all types of ethnic slurs over the years. Isaac was taken to his cell…Wow, you can imagine how uncomfortable he was when he was locked in this small compartment with a huge Swastika painted on the wall. Ironic, don't you think? A Jewish man locked in a jail cell with a Nazi symbol against the Jews painted on the wall and no place to go.

Isaac was schooled as an English major prior to attending nursing school. He had a ravenous appetite for reading. This is where God sends another twist, the ONLY reading material in the jail cell was a New Testament. The one book Isaac had avoided! God decided it was time for Isaac to read HIS WORD. Wherever Isaac was, he had a compulsion to read. He read the entire New Testament in one night, right there in the jail cell…alone, except being in the presence of Almighty God.

After Isaac's conviction for his DUI, he was forced to another mode of transportation for work. It was late summer, early fall in the Atlanta area, so riding a bicycle 30 miles seemed like a suitable option. He continued this cycling to get in better physical shape, until he was terminated from his job. Details of his termination are not necessary to understand the depths of low self esteem Isaac experienced. He was wallowing around in self-pity with little reason to feel optimistic about life. Isaac had gotten divorced a few years before and was not currently in a relationship.

Isaac was well liked by many of his coworkers. After working with the same people year after year, they became family. You accept one another for the quirks and encourage one another through life's challenges. Isaac went missing in action after his termination. The work crew would hear little about his well-being for weeks on end. Christian nurses prayed through the years for Isaac's salvation, that he would come to know of God's saving grace.

As an emergency department nurse, we worked any day of the week and weekend, any time of day or night as well as all holidays. The year Isaac faced major challenges, we knew God was at work. On Christmas day, while in the nurse's station, I watched our charge nurse Sarah answer the charge nurse phone as she did hundreds of times per day. She began with a smile, then a gasp as if she had heard the impossible. Tearfully Sarah handed the phone to a coworker and said Isaac wants to speak with you. One by one, the phone was handed to coworker after coworker, nurses, secretaries, technicians, and one by one Isaac (the Jewish guy) wished us "Merry Christmas" and informed us he had accepted Jesus Christ as his Savior in October. Coworkers were falling to their knees worshipping and praising Jesus. Some of these faithful saints had prayed for Isaac over an 18-year period.

Dear One, if you are brokenhearted about a loved one who has not come to know Christ, do NOT give up. Keep praying. God softened the heart of this haughty, pride-filled Jewish man and through the unending prayers of ones who loved Isaac, he is now trusting Jesus as his Savior. Hallelujah!!! God made what looked impossible, possible.

Matthew 19: 26 (NKJV)
But Jesus looked at them and said to them, "With men this is impossible, but with God all things are possible."

Mark 10: 27 (NKJV)
Jesus looked at them and said, "With men it is impossible, but not with God; for with God all things are possible."

Luke 1: 37 (NKJV)
"For with God nothing will be impossible"

Luke 18: 27 (NKJV)
The things which are impossible with men are possible with God

James 5: 16 (NKJV)
Confess your trespasses to one another and pray for one another that you may be healed. The effective, fervent prayer of a righteous man avails much.

Fervent means to keep a deep, focused, passion-filled heart on God. It means to align yourself with God. Even though Isaac was not ready to accept Jesus for many years, the passion filled Christian men and women he worked with kept their eyes and hearts focused on God. These coworkers loved Isaac enough to petition Almighty God on his behalf.

THE SHOWER

The all too familiar space…my shower…also known as my prayer closet. I have been here many times. I know what you are thinking…I do shower regularly. The space I am referring to is where I am the epitome of vulnerability…before Almighty God. I am stripped of any barrier my human self could possibly think of erecting.

How much more vulnerable can one be than naked before the Divine One? In a space, all alone, powerless, helpless, frail, feeble, crumbling—somewhere along the emotional/spiritual continuum between broken and whole.

This practice of meeting with Alpha and Omega in such a place began when my children were younger. Having six children in twelve years does not lend itself to much "me" time. Such time includes taking care of daily personal needs—showering and using the toilet. In the shower, behind closed doors, I could usually have time to enter the "inner chamber" and be open before God. My dear mother set such an honorable example of making sure she had time to meet with God free of distractions…ALONE.

Over the years, I have on more than one occasion been in the fetal position in the shower with water running over me…or clawing at the foggy doors as I wept bitterly begging God to have mercy on me. "I am so in need of You, Abba. I can't do this anymore" was my cry. For many moons my married life was in shambles. I had dreams shattered, been living in a destructive household with an abusive husband. I was incredibly miserable, having the life blood sucked out of me by any means he found available. So often, I tried to make it work while staying for the sake of the children.

As you read this, swallow your pride and admit, you have had similar thoughts. I know some of you have been in or are currently in ungodly, horrific circumstances. Many of you have suffered abuse…mental, emotional, physical, or sexual. Each circumstance causes enough trauma and confusion to swell up an entire universe of self-doubt and feeling like you are rudderless and worthless.

Many an ugly cry took place in the confines of what should provide refreshment and renewal on a regular basis. "Father, my soul is breaking… I'm shattering" as I lay face down trying to be thankful for what I had been given and uttering unabashed dependence on my Heavenly Father. "When will I feel loved? My friends are married and have loving supportive husbands. What is wrong with me?" At times, I was convinced my eyelids would permanently flip inside out because my anguish was so severe, my heartache so defeating.

I remember in January 2010, while in the shower, humbly asking God to forgive me because I was going to leave Andy. After 22 years of bickering and unloving behavior, I was preparing to leave. I knew God could get me through anything, but I could not take any more of living daily in abuse. I begged to be released from this snare. The abuse was emotional and mental for years, at the end it became physical. I could not stay…

In life, changes do not necessarily happen spontaneously. Life is a process full of events that must take place in the process. Life speeds up, slows down, and offers confusion, understanding, decisions, heartaches, anxiety, fears and consideration for everyone and everything involved. How, in the middle of this whirlwind, do I find God's will? His will for my life. His WILL for MY life. Let those words sink in…soak them up. My path is different from anyone else's path that has ever lived…hand woven by the Master. How do I know which way to turn? How do I know which way is right for me? Help me, Father…help me!!

During my healing process, God has taken me through a very lonely place. A location where He could deal with me. I have had dear friends walk away without explanation; I have had family not reach out when I needed support the most; I have been denied jobs I was more than qualified for because I do not compromise my values for the company. Coworkers barely speak to me because I am weird and do not fit in with the crowd. My encouragement to you is to NOT be afraid when God seeks to minister to you in the quietness and stillness of the healing process.

Psalm 46: 1-3 (NKJV)
God is our refuge and strength, a very present help in
trouble. Therefore we will not fear, even though the earth
be removed, and though the mountains be carried into the
midst of the sea; though its waters roar and be troubled,
though the mountains shake with its swelling.

Psalm 46: 10 (NKJV)
Be still, and know that I am God.

Isaiah 26: 3-4 (NKJV)
You will keep him in perfect peace, whose mind is stayed
on You, because He trusts in You. Trust in the Lord
forever, for in YAH, the Lord, the everlasting strength.

For some readers who are introverts, you are probably wishing for time
alone and a space where you can regroup. I need to let you know...that is
NOT me. On the pendulum of introvert on the left and extrovert on the
right, I sit on the part of the pendulum that is springing and bouncing way
passed the right border...so alone time is usually not my friend. Have to
say I have gotten MUCH better over the last several years.

Jesus went to an alone place to spend time with the Father. Bask in His
presence and listen for Him to console you and guide you.

YOU ARE ALONE

You are ALONE, are you listening? Look around you and recognize you ARE alone. You may be physically located in a busy shopping mall or heavily populated football game, but the enemy screams at you, "YOU ARE ALONE!" Holidays are especially difficult. Movies and television depict couples, happiness, and togetherness. Getting together often focuses on couples. How do you attend a social gathering with mainly couples, when you are single, without being reminded of how alone you are? How?

I am an extrovert and much of my recharging occurs when I spend time with family or friends. I get energized by my interactions with others. During my healing, God has taken me many places alone. I remember the first high school soccer game I attended, alone. It felt weird, but I did not cave in, I did not contract some dreaded illness, and I did not die. As I got past the self-consciousness of attending the game with no other family or friends sitting with me, I was able to enjoy watching Jake do what he did best—defense on the varsity soccer team.

No one was watching that I attended alone. I was the only one acutely aware of my loneliness. AH-HA, did you notice the change in words? I spoke of being alone, then I swapped to identify loneliness. I think back to the first time I attended a movie, in the theater, alone. And remembering the time I was the only one dining alone at a restaurant in a tiny town. I looked around at 45 other people at tables, no one dined alone…except me.

Satan shrieks "You are ALONE" as if it carries with it a dreaded curse, or sin. Satan would have you believe that being alone is never good. It has been my experience, when God takes you alone, He wishes to grow you. He wishes to spend intimate time with you, His child, to grow you in His ways, to display another dimension of His character to you personally. Have you seen God as your Provider? Your Husband? Your Sustainer?

Your Refuge? Your Confidant? If not, maybe it is time you see Him in these roles.

Being physically alone is one thing, since you are not expecting companionship, but being emotionally alone is a totally different animal. [During my marriage, I was commonly surrounded by loved ones physically (remember I have 6 children), but because of the dysfunction and lack of companionship with my spouse I was emotionally alone.] My husband and I slept in the same bed, rode together to many functions, and sat close to one another in church or school functions. This did not mean we were emotionally together or understanding the emotions of the other. Most days, the only emotion he could identify with was anger.

When I first married Andrew, I wholeheartedly believed I could share my deepest and darkest secrets with him. You know, the fears and snares we all face, the vulnerable crevices of our soul. I quickly discovered Andy could not be trusted with such information. He would resurface it to hurt me, tease me, or shame me into believing I was less than. This is not love. Over the years, I put up walls emotionally.

I sought refuge in the Scriptures, prayer, Bible studies, and communion with other Christians. By the time I left, I knew God could not use me fully inside this abusive marriage the way He could use me for His glory if I allowed Him to make me whole.

Dear Friend, I am not proposing divorce. I am proposing your relationship with Almighty God and His calling on your life come first—before relationship with a spouse, before relationship with your children, before your calling to be a missionary or nurse, before your career and before everything else.

Verses to read:

Isaiah 41:13 (NKJV)
For I, the Lord your God, will hold your right hand,
    Saying to you, "Fear not, I will help you."

Isaiah 46:4 (NKJV)
Even to your old age, I am He, and even to gray hairs I
will carry you!

I have made, and I will bear, even I will carry, and will deliver you.

Isaiah 49:15 & 16 (NKJV)
Can a woman forget her nursing child, and not have compassion on the son of her womb?
   Surely, they may forget, yet I will not forget you.
See, I have inscribed you on the palms of My hands,
   Your walls are continually before Me.

Psalm 63:8 (NKJV)
My soul follows close behind You.
   Your right hand upholds me.

Psalm 73:23 & 24 (NKJV)
Nevertheless, I am continually with You; You hold me by my right hand,
You will guide me with Your counsel, and afterward receive me to glory.

Psalm 139:10 (NKJV)
Even there Your hand shall lead me,
   And Your right hand shall hold me.

Matthew 22:37-38 (NKJV)
Jesus said to him, "You shall love the Lord your God with all your heart, with all your soul, and with all your mind. This is the first and great commandment."

Deuteronomy 31:8 (ESV)
And the LORD, He is the One who goes before you. He will be with you, He will not leave you nor forsake you; do not fear nor be dismayed.
Listen to these songs:
Just Be Held by Casting Crowns
I Am Not Alone by Kari Jobe

WHO YOU SAY I AM

Who are you? Yes, I asked the question. Who are you? Maybe you are a mother, a daughter, a son, a friend. Maybe you are a preacher, a teacher, a baseball hero, or drug addict. But who are you…really?

I would venture to say I am not the only one who has struggled with a definition of me as I go through my life. Let's see, I have been a daughter, a scholar, an athlete, a nurse, a wife, a mother, a friend, and a sister. I have also been a student, a teacher, a follower, and a leader. I have been a sinner and some have seen me as a saint. I have been a failure in many ways and many categories. I have fallen short in as many or more categories as I have rallied.

None of these roles, positions, or titles matter compared to what God thinks of you. He sees your heart. He knows more about you than you do about yourself, more than your parents or spouse. He is looking for your surrender, in attitude and spirit, actions and words. He is looking for your obedience and total trust in Him. He desires your confession of dependency on Him.

Please take a few minutes to read through the lyrics of *Who You Say I Am,* and at some point take time to listen to this powerful song by Hillsong Worship.

Who You Say I Am
<u>Hillsong Worship</u>

You are for me, not against me
I am who You say I am
I am who You say I am
Who the Son sets free

Oh is free indeed
I'm a child of God, yes, I am

Satan lashes out when we are close to God. If Satan is beating the tar out of you, you can rest assured you are doing something right in God's eyes.

Years ago, in my civilian job, our department got a new director, Natalie. She appeared professional, wore business suits and pumps with dignity. She had an impressive CV, not a resume because she was too educated. A few months passed, she hired a bunch of scalawags with no manners and no professionalism. That is a hard pill to swallow when you work at the "uptown hospital" in an affluent section of old money Atlanta.

Natalie continued to show her true colors and reveal in a very distasteful way, she was an alcoholic. Her judgment was clouded and her interpersonal skills lacking. She said some inflammatory words to me and imposed illegal stipulations on my position. What was I going to do? Could I fight? I did some soul searching, Bible reading and then I began to pray.

Feeling my earthly options were limited, I was obedient to God's word. Less than two weeks before my birthday, I began to pray. I prayed fervently. My brother-in-law conducted Bible readings and prayer in his home EVERY morning. I spent summers of my growing up years, from age 8 to 18, at his home. Every morning he prayed 1 Timothy 2: 1-3

1 Timothy 2:1 (NKJV)
First of all, then, I urge that supplications, prayers, intercessions, and thanksgivings be made of all people for kings and all who are in high positions, that we may lead a peaceful and quiet life, godly and dignified in every way.
this is good, and it is pleasing in the sight of God our Savior.

I took heed of these words. I prayed out of obedience. I was resting on the fact I belonged to Jesus, I am His. Because I belong to Him, I cling to His definition of who I am. I prayed and prayed, not out of love for my director but out of love for Christ. I confessed before the Lord, "I don't know how to pray this, but Your WORD instructs me to pray for those who are in authority over me…so that is what I am doing. I am praying for the director and the position of authority she has."

Guess what, the week of my birthday, the director was terminated and escorted off hospital property by security.

Pay attention. I did not pray anything specific would happen. I did not pray for her termination. I prayed for her as an authority figure because the Bible tells me this is what I should do. I had no idea God would terminate her the week of my birthday. Happy Birthday, Stella!

Fast forward a year:

A coworker, Lennie, who portrayed herself as a friend began to commit more and more acts against me. She would report lies to our next new director, Robert, and present the information in a most convincing manner. Robert would in turn approach me with prejudice and confront me with accusations. From my perspective, I was clueless because Lennie was fabricating information.

The problem I faced was Lennie was quite the manipulator and department influencer. For part of the time we worked together, she was my immediate supervisor. The tension built and built. My coworkers noticed how Lennie lashed out at me. What was I to do? I learned something the previous year, so I began to pray. I prayed that God would handle Lennie, I was at a loss as to how to manage my relationship with my coworker Lennie and my director Robert.

Guess what? One day I was on the treadmill at the gym and my good friend Ann called. She asked my whereabouts and then instructed me to exit the treadmill. She did not want me to hurt myself because she had something to tell me. Lennie had been terminated. It was less than 2 weeks before Christmas. Merry Christmas, Stella!

Please understand, I am not making light of these situations. I was shocked and amazed at God's timing for each incident. Also notice, I did not pray for their demise. Everyone needs a job. I surrendered and was obedient. God did everything else and His timing was perfect.

God will allow his children to be tested. When He sees that enough of the trial has occurred, He will make your enemies your footstool. (***The Lord said to my Lord, "sit at my right hand, Till I make Your enemies***

Your footstool." Psalm 110:1 NKJV) I had chosen to draw close to the Lord, I had chosen to be obedient to Him and seek my identity in the Lord. He in turn vanquished my foe. In other words, God Himself conquered my enemy.

WHEN YOUR ENTIRE WORLD IS CAVING IN #2

Scenario #2: You're an active woman in her mid 40's, a bunch of kids and decent career. You've been married to someone you once loved dearly, but he does not return your care and affection. Oh, there is plenty of action in the bedroom, thus the "bunch of kids". But the tenderness, compassion and awareness of your emotional well-being does not exist. You married him because you loved him. You thought he loved you, too. He said he did.

Your childhood home was not all unicorns and rainbows, and you knew marriage could be challenging. Your father was an alcoholic and emotionally abusive to your mother, but they "loved each other". Right? You witnessed and experienced intense financial hardship and had a bird's eye view of doing without. Even doing without necessities, like shoes which lacked holes in the bottom. This was your limited childhood perspective of owning your own business. Therefore, as you reached adulthood, being an entrepreneur was never a goal. You sought a steady, dependable bi-weekly paycheck with benefits.

How did you marry someone without this same perspective? Shoulder shrug. How did you miss his inability to submit to authority? For example, amiably working for someone. Young and coming from a skewed viewpoint, I guess. You were missing some tools in the toolbox of healthy life relationships.

You did your best. You kept going through the motions of what you thought a marriage should be. You cleaned the house, with little help from your hubby. You cooked for everyone. You worked weekend night shift so you could be with your kids during the week and make the most money with the shortest number of hours worked. You took the kids to church and insisted as long as you could for them to attend Christian school. You wanted them to have a solid foundation in Christianity. Somehow as the years passed, your efforts were not enough. Would they ever be enough?

After 17 years of marriage, you realized your husband's maternal grandmother had been more of a mother to him than his own mother. Why did this information not reveal itself earlier? You were figuring out he did not have the capacity to love nor a correct understanding of love. His mother did not love him the way a little boy needed to be loved in those formative years. His father worked many hours in your husband's young years, but your husband's mother did not provide the comfort, affection and love your husband needed. How had you missed this glaring discrepancy? How can he love you when he does not love himself? How can he love your children when he doesn't love himself? How can he love himself when he doesn't know how? Can you go the rest of your life in a marriage that does not contain love? And it does contain abuse. Abusive language toward you, destructive and violent behavior in the home, how can you continue? When do you leave and what are the consequences?

You had removed your wedding ring when you were pregnant with child #4, your husband never noticed. After delivering this precious little daughter, you never resumed wearing the wedding ring because you realized your marriage wasn't quite a marriage. Yet you stayed. The verbal abuse got worse as the years went by. Is this a reason for divorce? NO ONE in your family gets divorced, and the Bible speaks against divorce.

You kept doing more and more, the house, the yard, working overtime and he made less and less money, contributed less and resented every step you took. Now that a few more years have passed, you have two more children. You and hubby are up to a total of six living and two miscarriages. You grieved the loss, he never did. He never would speak of the babies you lost. You grieved this alone. You work harder and harder, the money got stretched tighter and tighter, yet he contributed little. He insisted on discussing the bills, then would give his input on what the bill paying priorities would be, turn and walk away with no financial contribution.

Is this for better or for worse? His words toward you become harsher, more degrading. He tells you "You're no fun anymore". Fun? How can you be fun when you are so exhausted by all the responsibilities and no help from him? He repeatedly quizzes you with "what man would ever want you? The mother of six children," as if you had the ugly plague written all over your face and body like a flashing neon sign.

Who would want you? You bear scars of bearing many children, you carried each one to full term and your body shows the stretch marks. Certain body parts did not return to their original location. You breastfed for six years of your life. You would do it again to have six healthy children. Is there a man who will love you? You are filled with doubts, you become full of resentment. You and hubby have been to counseling, separately and marriage counseling. You have been on marriage retreats only to have him not participate in the groundwork and then wonder why you leave the retreat disappointed and dejected.

Trapped is a pretty good descriptive word to capture the feeling of this mid 40's woman. Numb is another good one. Then the abuse escalated. Dishes were broken, bookshelves overturned, holes punched in walls—in front of the children. Later you discover this fractures their thought processes and causes long lasting emotional trauma. Had you known, you probably would have tried to leave earlier.

Where do you go? How do you decide it's the right time? Hubby steals money from the checking account via the ATM, he forges checks on an account that only bears your name. How can you survive and pay the bills if this behavior continues? You must get out.

You are working as a youth worker at the church. One Wednesday evening, the youth pastor preaches "If you want to walk on water, you gotta get outta the boat". These words you heard quite distinctly. They reverberated in your head, your heart, and your soul for the remainder of the week. That next weekend your entire family traveled to Virginia to spend time with a friend of your hubby. You attended church that Sunday, way on top of a hill. The preacher preached "If you want to walk on water, you gotta get outta the boat". At this point you can hardly believe your ears. You are so miserable in your marriage, could God be telling you when to leave?

The Sunday after Virginia, hubby decided the entire family should travel about an hour away from home to attend a church. The pastor there was fiery and energetic, pounced around the stage demonstratively. You will never forget his sermon that day, "If you want to walk on water, you gotta get outta the boat". This was God giving you permission of when to leave this life of destruction and chaos—the abuse. God had plans for you, and you had to step out in faith.

Then it happens, nearly 22 years into the marriage. You have been wrestling with leaving for years. You had read through 14 years of your journals which revealed you were living the definition of insanity. You were going through the same motions, with the same person, and expecting a different result. You have had enough and inform him, "I do not wish to be your wife another minute, another day, another month, another year." You didn't yell, you said it with calmness and total resolve. He was shocked.

Did he perceive the marriage as good? How could he? World War III, IV and V occurred on a cyclic rotation about every 3 weeks. The conflict always struck when you were exhausted from working the weekend when your resilience was at its lowest. You had little sleep in three days due to working the night shift. A common week would have you awake from Friday morning to Saturday morning including the 12-hour night shift in the emergency department where you were in charge of making life and death decisions the entire 12 hours. Let us not forget the hour-long drive to and from work.

You are getting older, this cannot continue. Hubby was upset at the thought of you leaving. He even mentioned, if you had informed him five years sooner, he would have willingly just walked away because he was so miserable. WHY did he not give you the memo?!!! You had been contemplating leaving for six years. Big sigh!!! Timing seems to always be out of whack. Another big sigh!!!

How do you divide stuff? Which child goes with which parent? Questions? Questions? This was not a decision you reached easily. It was through much prayer, consternation and a cascade of endless tears that got you to this point. As the months went by until you moved out, hubby got even more abusive. He threw your pocketbook out in the front yard, flinging its contents on the yard. Not lawn because you could never maintain a lawn without his help. You had too much burden on your shoulders.

There were many outbursts. One night, you were tossed about in the laundry room by him, ending up with scratches and bruises on your body. This was less than two weeks after you met with the attorney to start the divorce process. The three youngest witnessed the encounter and your second oldest pulled hubby away from you.

Another night stands out from the rest. Hubby was upset about you leaving, the yelling began and then his violent eruption occurred in your bedroom. As you sat on the edge of the bed, he proceeded to destroy the bedroom. He overturned every piece of furniture except the bed where you sat—he overturned the armoire with his clothing and TV cabinet. He yanked the ceiling fan out of the ceiling and tore the door off the hinges. The peace that passes all understanding was with you in that space. Your heartbeat did not rise, you did not raise your voice or provide harsh words. You calmly uttered, "and you wonder why I want to leave". Thankfully five of the six children were spending the night with friends. Your comfort and strength came from the Lord. This was supernatural peace, not what you could muster amid the violence and chaos. God totally protected you and held your tongue. Had you struck out verbally, that night might have been your last.

Methodically you gathered your belongings and placed what you could in storage so when THE day to leave arrived, you would have no obstruction. At least that is what you tried to do. When the day came, he was angry, calling you all kinds of names in front of the children. You had rented a truck to help with heavier objects.

The oldest was at college, the two boys who followed stayed with Dad and you took the three younger ones to the new rental house. That evening felt so heavy. You unloaded what you could before everyone was too tired. You needed to feed your young ones. The solemness with which you attempted to eat even a bite, was too much to bear. Yes, you had been abused. Yes, you wanted better for you and your children. But you are the one who left. Are you wearing the weight of a Scarlet Letter on your chest so everyone in town can see that YOU are the one who walked out of your marriage? Would you be seen as the one who abandoned the relationship?

You find yourself alone. Your mom calls to check on you, but she does not agree with you divorcing your husband. Your siblings do not reach out to check on you. Thankfully, you have many dear friends who care and want you to be okay. Half of your church family has nothing to do with you. A few grace-filled church members show up bearing gifts.

One brought a bed for you. A college friend gave you a dining table and six chairs. Your new neighbors watched your children while you worked.

Everywhere you turn, you are reminded you are ALONE. News flash, you were ALONE in your marriage only it was screaming at you and not at those on the outside. Everywhere you go, you are reminded you are ALONE. It is as if the universe cries out, bellows at times "you are ALONE".

You are not alone; Jesus is with you. You turn to Him, and He provides peace, comfort, and the love you desperately need. You absorb yourself in His word and bask in His presence. You cry and grieve, not because you miss hubby. You grieve for the relationship that never was, but should have been. You tried, you gave it your best, and your best was not good enough.

Take the time God decides is enough time to heal. Time for your children to heal and mature. Even time for your ex-husband to heal and settle where he no longer lashes out at you. He will never change. If he enjoyed upsetting you when you were married, that trait does not go away with time. Set appropriate boundaries and walk away. Do not fall prey to his cunning ways.

The following verses helped to sustain me through these dark times:

Romans 5:8 (NKJV)
But God demonstrates His own love toward us, in that while we were still sinners, Christ died for us.

1 Corinthians 10:13 (NKJV)
No temptation has overtaken you except such as is common to man; but God *is* faithful, who will not allow you to be tempted beyond what you are able, but with the temptation will also make the way of escape, that you may be able to bear *it.*

Matthew 14:22-33 (NKJV)
Jesus Walks on the Sea

[22] Immediately Jesus [a]made His disciples get into the boat and go before Him to the other side, while He sent the

55

multitudes away. [23] And when He had sent the multitudes away, He went up on the mountain by Himself to pray. Now when evening came, He was alone there. [24] But the boat was now [b]in the middle of the sea, tossed by the waves, for the wind was contrary.

[25] Now in the fourth watch of the night Jesus went to them, walking on the sea. [26] And when the disciples saw Him walking on the sea, they were troubled, saying, "It is a ghost!" And they cried out for fear.

[27] But immediately Jesus spoke to them, saying, [c]"Be of good cheer! [d]It is I; do not be afraid."

[28] And Peter answered Him and said, "Lord, if it is You, command me to come to You on the water."

[29] So He said, "Come." And when Peter had come down out of the boat, he walked on the water to go to Jesus. [30] But when he saw [e]that the wind *was* boisterous, he was afraid; and beginning to sink he cried out, saying, "Lord, save me!"

[31] And immediately Jesus stretched out *His* hand and caught him, and said to him, "O you of little faith, why did you doubt?" [32] And when they got into the boat, the wind ceased.

[33] Then those who were in the boat [f]came and worshiped Him, saying, "Truly You are the Son of God."

The verses correspond to the following song. I played this song over and over, played it loud and sang it until I was hoarse.

Voice of Truth By Casting Crowns

Choosing to listen and believe the Voice of Truth made ALL the difference in the world. God demonstrated His love and compassion toward me over and over. He prompted older godly women from my former church to send kind notes in the mail, arriving when I needed them most. He kept my longstanding girlfriends beside me, encouraging me and helping me move forward. He provided me with the best neighbor I ever had—she became like a sister to me and was more than willing to help oversee my children. She knew I was a single parent and doing my best to survive and provide for my babies.

Statistically, a woman will attempt to leave an abusive relationship up to seven times before she gets out...if she ever gets out. The scars for her and her children can be long-lasting, but by God's grace they all can be okay.

THE STRENGTH

Where does it come from? How does it keep coming? Why don't I "feel" strong? Repeatedly I'm approached by individuals who tell me "You are so strong". Why do I feel like I am falling apart?

I fall before God's throne, I ask Him to give me the strength to put one foot in front of the other. Looking back, when my children were little and our house was three stories, I was so exhausted but needed to discipline a wee one once again before my head hit the pillow, pouring out my supplication before the Lord..." help me... a few more minutes...give me strength to tell Jake and Tuck one more time." "Father, I can't do this anymore, I just can't. I'm so tired I can't breathe. I certainly do not have the strength to correct behavior AGAIN tonight...help me."

> 2 Corinthians 12: 7-10
> And lest I should be exalted above measure by the abundance of the revelations, a thorn in the flesh was given to me, a messenger of Satan to buffet me, lest I be exalted above measure. Concerning this thing I pleaded with the Lord three times that it might depart from me. And He said to me, "My grace is sufficient for you, for My strength is made perfect in weakness." Therefore, most gladly I will rather boast in my infirmities, that the power of Christ may rest upon me. Therefore, I take pleasure in infirmities, in reproaches, in needs, in persecutions, in distresses, for Christ's sake. For when I am weak, then I am strong.

How can others see my strength? I am crumbling daily, sometimes shattered with my head barely out of the ditch. My prayers might not be long. Many times, I have whispered, "Lord, help me." At one of the facilities where I worked for decades, I was in charge of a relatively busy emergency department. Patients were consistently and rapidly presenting by private car and by ambulance. This facility cared for a medically complicated population. The housekeeper, Jason, would come to me after the department had an intensely busy period and remark how calm I was during the entire chaotic time. What I knew is God allowed Jason to see calm during the storm when my insides where quite stormy. During the storm, I had cried out in my spirit for God to calm me, to help me make wise decisions and help us get to a better part of the shift. My response to Jason was consistently, "I'm thankful that calmness is what God allows you to see." You have most likely heard of the duck looking calm on the surface but paddling like crazy underneath the water. This was me in the middle of the storms at work.

"Be strong and courageous. Do not be afraid or terrified because of them, for the LORD your God goes with you; He will never leave you or forsake you." Deuteronomy 31: 6 Because the Israelites needed encouragement, just a few verses later God repeats, "The LORD Himself goes before you and will be with you; He will never leave you nor forsake you. Do not be afraid; do not be discouraged." Oh, how I cling to these verses and utter them softly when I find myself overwhelmed.

Thank You LORD for allowing others to see Your strength and peace through me.

Thank You LORD for bringing each of us through the storm. Thank You LORD for being You.

LORD, I WILL GO

Have you ever needed a change? Do you know which category of your life needs change? Is it work? Is it a geographical location? Have you been working the same job, month after month, year after year? Have you lived in the same area for 20 years?

I was stuck. Stuck in the type of job I love, emergency nursing, but not feeling fulfilled or appreciated. Oh, there were a handful of staff who appreciated me, but there were more than a handful that made my work life a living hell.

I began to pray, "Lord, if You will send me…I will go." With this prayer, I did not specify any location or any type of job placement. I prayed for months, over and over, "Lord, if You will send me…I will go." What I did not realize was God had all kinds of things in motion I could not see. I started writing a book years ago, but did not get very far. I was feeling the burden of writing, but when would my head be free of chaos long enough to be creative?

When I left for northern North Dakota, I knew one person who was working in that area. I knew God directed me to this location, but I did not know why. What I did know, my one friend in North Dakota was home grown and would help me any way he could if I needed it. If I had car trouble, he would help. If I needed help finding accommodation, he would help. He is just good people.

I grew up and lived my life in the southeastern United States with mild winters and hot humid summers. God was taking me to a whole new world, the frozen tundra where winter lasts for six months. For the first four months I did not see the concrete sidewalks or asphalt roadways due to the thick ice on the surfaces.

Some would consider the conditions stark and uninviting, but for me it was an opportunity. But there I could possibly find enough empty mind space to pen the book God was nudging me to write. If you read *Touched by an Angel,* you know I soon discovered a publishing company on Main Street of this tiny town.

To add to God's mission for me, the week I recognized the publishing company was only a few blocks away, I received an email from a different publishing company. Ladies and gentlemen, are you reading correctly? I did not write that I reached out to a publishing company, the publishing company reached out to me!!! It was a Christian publishing company and when I spoke with a representative, she encouraged me.

If this is not enough, two weeks after I was contacted by the publishing company I spoke with my long-time friend from the military, retired Chief Master Sergeant Chambers. He was willing to edit my writings prior to sending them to the publisher. Are you holding onto yourself? Chambers had recently finished his doctorate in English and knows my story. There is no one who can convince me that God is not orchestrating the writing of this book.

Psalm 37: 23-24 (NKJV)
The steps of a good man are ordered by the LORD, and He delights in his way.
Though he fall, he shall not be utterly cast down; for the Lord upholds him with his hand.

There is not one day of our lives that takes God by surprise.

Proverbs 16: 3 and 9 (NKJV)
Commit your works to the Lord, and your thoughts will be established.
A man's heart plans his way, but the Lord directs his steps.

Proverbs 2: 1-9 (NKJV)
My son, if you receive my words, and treasure my commands within you,
So that you incline your ear to wisdom, and apply your heart to understanding;

Yes, if you cry out for discernment, and lift up your voice for understanding,

If you seek her as silver, and search for her as for hidden treasures;

Then you will understand the fear of the Lord, and find the knowledge of God.

For the Lord gives wisdom; from His mouth come knowledge and understanding;

He stores up sound wisdom for the upright; He is a shield to those who walk uprightly;

He guards the paths of justice, and preserves the way of His saints.

Then you will understand righteousness and justice, equity and every good path.

Proverbs 3: 5-8 (NKJV)
Trust in the Lord with all your heart, and lean not on your own understanding

In all your ways acknowledge Him, and He shall direct your paths.

Do not be wise in your own eyes; fear the Lord and depart from evil.

It will be health to your flesh, and strength to your bones.

John 10: 14-15, 27 (NKJV)
"I am the good shepherd; and I know My sheep, and am known by My own.

As the Father knows Me, even so I know the Father, and I lay down My life for the sheep.

My sheep hear My voice, and I know them, and they follow Me."

1 Thessalonians 5: 16-23 (NKJV)
Rejoice always,
Pray without ceasing,

In everything give thanks; for this is the will of God in Christ Jesus for you.

Do not quench the Spirit.

Do not despise prophecies,

Test all things; hold fast what is good.

Abstain from every form of evil.

Now may the God of peace Himself sanctify you completely; and may your whole spirit, soul and body be preserved blameless at the coming of our Lord Jesus Christ.

HELP ME SEE

Heavenly Father,

I bow before You, on bended knee. I am incredibly thankful for Your blessings: my children (six of them),

my grandchildren,

my health,

my ability to work at my age and make money,

my multitude of friends

a great education and college degrees

Help me, Father, for I am crumbling before You. I desire companionship. I really tried with Andy, but it was not meant to be. Am I that unlovable? Am I that undesirable? There is a void that all the children and grandchildren in the world cannot fill. I am only human. You made me a tactile being who is and has been physically alone. How is this good?

I am a mere human who is physically and emotionally...alone. I have longed to share my life with that special someone, even before I met Andy. But God, in Your wisdom, have me alone on this part of my journey—without that special someone holding my hand or kissing me goodnight. How long? I am trying to understand and to be patient.

I desire touch and emotional intimacy. I desire to be in relationship, to be happily married. Why must I wait? So long? Not just months, or years, we are past a decade now. Lord, have You forgotten me? Lord, please have mercy. I know, with Your help I can be a good wife. I was a good wife to Andy. Can I please be in a relationship? How is it good for me to be without affection so long?

Deep breath and long sigh.

Stella, you want to catapult forward yet shattered family members stand before you and reassure you that you are exactly where God would have you be. You are not where you want to be, but His ways are higher than our human ways. God has you where you can serve Him and serve His people to bring glory to His Name.

I feel quite discouraged, yet ashamed at the same time. I am not trying to be selfish. Father, purge any ungodly attitudes in me. Father, forgive me if I am being selfish. Please help me to see Your perspective. Help me to see with Your loving eyes of discernment.

Help me Father, in Jesus Holy and Precious Name. The Name above ALL names.

Amen

♡

SAUDADE PART 3

My oldest daughter Amy finished her Master's degree as a social worker and completed her classroom, practicum, and testing to be a licensed clinical social worker (LCSW). She knew from age 10 she was called to foster and adopt children. One night she called me and whispering as to not wake her husband, she told me as she goes through her house "someone is missing". I shared the word and meaning of "saudade" with her. It was the term she was looking for.

The months went by, and Amy kept waiting for the void to be filled. She had fostered a few children for varying periods of time, but none were her saudade. It wasn't until the babies came that Amy was fulfilled. She allowed me to read the part of her dissertation pertaining to their arrival and how she experienced a connectedness to D within the first 24 hours of his arrival in her home. K took a little longer. Funny observation we each had is K had a personality that mimicked Amy's.

D and K were with Amy, her husband Brannon, and their daughter Grace for over 18 months before the court decided that reunification with biological parents was appropriate.

Fast forward a year

The separation was rough, well actually unbearable. Brannon offered no emotional support for Amy as she grieved intolerably. Amy had lost D at the beginning of September and K six weeks later, just four days before K turned two. Amy had been the only Mama K had known. From Amy's perspective, how do you carry on? Imagine how alone she felt without the support of Brannon. Most days she was in a fog just trying to survive. As she fell asleep each night, she felt her heart shattering with this great loss.

Amy had forgiven Brannon for much over the years. He had violated their marriage time after time. Looking back, Amy realizes the babies had to leave when they did so she would have the ability to divorce Brannon.

Through conversations and time well spent, Amy has established an ongoing healthy relationship with D and K's biological parents. Amy and Grace are regularly invited to birthday parties, D and K were thrilled to attend Grace's party as well. This must be the miracle we were waiting for and could not see. D and K have returned to what once was a violent home, but now it is not. D and K are growing and thriving. Grace and her siblings enjoy each moment spent together.

Praise the Lord, praise the Lord, praise the Lord. D and K will always be our "babies", and yes, they get birthday and Christmas presents from their non-biological grandmother. The current situation is healthy, respectful, and loving for the babies. It is made possible by the GRACE of God.

When I visit Amy, her refrigerator is filled with pictures, old and new, of her with Grace, D and K. I am thankful God is healing my daughter's heart by allowing her to still have D and K in her life. God can bless us beyond our imagination. He makes BEAUTY from ASHES every day… we must pay attention to His work.

Verses to read:

Isaiah 61 (NKJV)
The Spirit of the Lord God is upon me, because the Lord has anointed me
to bring good news to the poor, he has sent me to bind up the brokenhearted,
to proclaim liberty to the captives, and the opening of the prison to those who are bound;
to proclaim the year of the LORD's favor, and the day of vengeance of our God; to comfort all who mourn;
to grant to those who mourn in Zion—
to give them a beautiful headdress instead of ashes, the oil of gladness instead of mourning, the garment of praise instead of a faint spirit; that they may be called oaks of righteousness, the planting of the LORD, that He may be glorified.
They shall build up the ancient ruins;

They shall rise up the former devastations;
They shall repair the ruined cities,
The devastations of many generations.
Strangers shall stand and tend your flocks;
Foreigners shall be your plowmen and vinedressers;
but you shall be called the priests of the LORD;
They shall speak of you as the ministers of our God;
You shall eat the wealth of the nations, and in their glory,
you shall boast.

1 Instead of your shame there shall be a double portion; instead of dishonor they shall rejoice in their lot; therefore in their land they shall possess a double portion; they shall have everlasting joy.
2 For I the LORD love justice; I hate robbery and wrong; I will faithfully give them their recompense, and I will make an everlasting covenant with them. 9 Their offspring shall be known among the nations, and their descendants in the midst of the peoples; all who see them shall acknowledge them, that they are an offspring the LORD has blessed.
10 I will greatly rejoice in the LORD;
My soul shall exult in my God,
For He has clothed me with the garments of salvation; He has covered me with the robe of righteousness, as a bridegroom decks himself like a priest with a beautiful headdress, and as a bride adorns herself with her jewels. 11 For as the earth brings forth its sprouts, and as a garden causes what is sown in it to sprout up, so the LORD GOD will cause righteousness and praise to sprout up before all the nations.

I encourage you to listen to the song "Just Be Held" performed by Casting Crowns.

WHO KNEW? PART I

I had gone through many years of my life with a desire to serve in the United States military. After I turned 35 and quit receiving advertisements soliciting my membership, the thoughts of ever serving drifted away. I was busy working and raising my six children.

One Wednesday evening after church, my good friend asked if I had ever considered joining the military. This sparked my interest, and I began to reach out to the different branches. I determined the particulars of each branch and what we could offer each other, settling on the Air National Guard.

In my mid-40's, I raised my right hand and swore to protect the US Constitution against all enemies foreign or domestic. Due to my greater than 20 years as a civilian nurse, I commissioned as a Major. Wow! would not recommend. It comes with a steep learning curve. I did not even know how to wear my uniform correctly. Lord have mercy.

I loved what I did as a nurse in the Guard. Loved my chief nurse and the work she pulled me into. We were part of a disaster team for Homeland Security, joining forces with the Army Guard. We had numerous field exercises and sweat our way through equipment sets at the Armory, determining best practice for field operations.

The construct of our unit changed as the years went by, positions changed but the mission remained. I had poured my sweat and tears into this mission for quite some time. With the changes, I was pushed to the side. Defeated, I wasn't sure where I fit in.

Our executive committee met to discuss strategies of the coming months. As I arrived at the meeting, I was informed I had been chosen as the deputy commander of the team (Battalion level). I wasn't even present for the discussion. God works in crazy ways.

When I commissioned, the position did not exist. Later I discovered, I was the first Air Force member to hold this title in the Nation. Just when I thought I was topsy turvy and not knowing next steps, God had a plan all along.

Stay tuned for Peanut Butter and Jelly…and more.

Psalm 37: 23-24
The Lord directs the steps of the godly. He delights in every detail of their lives. Though they stumble, they will never fall, for the Lord holds them by the hand.

Proverbs 16: 9
A man's heart plans his way, but the LORD directs his steps.

Psalm 31: 14-15
But I trust in you, Lord; I say, "You are my God, My times are in your hands."

Proverbs 20: 24
The Lord directs our steps, so why try to understand everything along the way?

Psalm 119: 105
Your WORD is a lamp unto my feet and a light unto my path.

Proverbs 19: 21
Many are the plans in a person's heart, but it is the Lord's purpose that prevails.

Isaiah 48: 17
Thus says the LORD, your Redeemer, The Holy One of Israel;
I am the LORD your God, who teaches you to profit,
Who leads you by the way you should go.

WHO KNEW? PART II

Being chosen as the deputy commander of the Battalion, I was interested in meeting the commander. I had not heard his name, though many others knew him well. I received a phone call from LtCol Stephens recommending we meet face-to-face considering we would be working together.

He chose the place, and we would meet for lunch on Friday. As the day approached, I decided it was necessary to take my youngest daughter with me to lunch and continue my trek to match up with my oldest daughter halfway between her Florida residence and mine in Georgia.

I reached out to LtCol Stephens, who agreed to having my daughter Elisabeth join us. As Lizzy and I drove to the restaurant, I advised her teenage self that it was an important military business meeting, and I would appreciate all the common courtesies from her. I pondered how the meeting would go, what kind of a person will I be serving with? I was talking to God and noted, "it sure would be cool if LtCol Stephens is a Christian. I just think things will go smoother for me."

Arriving at the restaurant, he was of course early like any true Army dude. As we approached the table, LtCol Stephens stood up in a gentlemanly manner, extended his hand to shake mine with the greeting, "Hi my name is Stephens and I'm a believer in Jesus Christ." Well, ain't God good? That was one of the fastest answers to prayer I had ever seen. Maybe ten minutes.

Who knew?

Psalm 121
I will lift up my eyes to the hills—from whence comes my help? My help comes from the Lord, who made heaven and earth.

He will not allow your foot to be moved; He who keeps you will not slumber. Behold, He who keeps Israel shall neither slumber nor sleep.

The Lord is your keeper; the Lord is your shade at your right hand. The sun shall not strike you by day, nor the moon by night.

The Lord shall preserve you from all evil; He shall preserve your soul. The Lord shall preserve your going out and your coming in from this time forth, and even forevermore.

♡
WHO KNEW PART III

As I began to serve with LtCol Stephens, we had a natural bond. I attribute it to our relationship with the Lord, making us brother and sister in Christ. Our personalities are so different, yet complimentary. Our backgrounds are entirely dissimilar—he has been career non-medical military and I have been career medical civilian until later in life. I refer to our kinship as peanut butter and jelly.

While I had a full-time civilian job, LtCol Stephens incorporated me into the staff meetings as much as possible, especially those leading up to a field exercise. I was shown the utmost respect by my Army counterparts and embraced into the enterprise smoothly.

LtCol Stephens would frequently ask clarifying questions—"is this a medical thing?" or "is this how the Air Force does it?" "Help me understand". We made it through the growing pains together. Army and Air Force working together to reach a common goal in the realm of disaster preparedness. While we did have conversations, there were many hours spent walking a footprint, interacting with troops where barely a word was spoken between us and somehow the understanding of operations existed. We both learned a lot.

Respect and appreciation for the talents of the other permeated our two and a half years together. I remember one exercise; I was getting flack from my ex-husband. I don't play poker well, so Stephens could tell I was not right. I, on the other hand, was attempting to keep my military bearing in front of the Battalion. Stephens approached me, full of compassion although clad in his Army uniform, combat boots, shaved head, and stern facial expression. To not cry in front of others, I kept my head up and eyes up so the tears would not blip over the edge.

After the days exercise when I could speak with Stephens privately,

I confessed the static I was receiving from my ex. He admitted he knew something was wrong and offered to pray with me. I further explained I was about to cry earlier and knew that was unbecoming for my position. My brother-in-Christ said, I am here for you as your brother-in-Christ, I will pray with you and for you at any time. You see, in the body of Christ, we walk together through the good times and the bad, through the victories and the yuckiness of life.

LtCol Stephens and I needed each other like peanut butter and jelly.

1 Corinthians 12:12-27
English Standard Version
One Body with Many Members

[12] For just as the body is one and has many members, and all the members of the body, though many, are one body, so it is with Christ. [13] For in one Spirit we were all baptized into one body—Jews or Greeks, slaves[a] or free—and all were made to drink of one Spirit.

[14] For the body does not consist of one member but of many. [15] If the foot should say, "Because I am not a hand, I do not belong to the body," that would not make it any less a part of the body. [16] And if the ear should say, "Because I am not an eye, I do not belong to the body," that would not make it any less a part of the body. [17] If the whole body were an eye, where would be the sense of hearing? If the whole body were an ear, where would be the sense of smell? [18] But as it is, God arranged the members in the body, each one of them, as he chose. [19] If all were a single member, where would the body be? [20] As it is, there are many parts,[b] yet one body.

[21] The eye cannot say to the hand, "I have no need of you," nor again the head to the feet, "I have no need of you." [22] On the contrary, the parts of the body that seem to be weaker are indispensable, [23] and on those parts

of the body that we think less honorable we bestow the greater honor, and our unpresentable parts are treated with greater modesty, [24] which our more presentable parts do not require. But God has so composed the body, giving greater honor to the part that lacked it, [25] that there may be no division in the body, but that the members may have the same care for one another. [26] If one member suffers, all suffer together; if one member is honored, all rejoice together.

[27] Now you are the body of Christ and individually members of it.

WHO KNEW PART IV

You have no idea what influence you have on those who cross your path. Many individuals are quite observant when you have no clue they are watching.

LtCol Stephens invited me to his home to meet his wife and participate in Bible study. Remember a great deal of our time together on mission was quiet. I was learning much about being a field commander and he was processing information.

As I arrived at the Stephens' home, I was introduced to all the others attending. It became quickly evident that I was the only one who knew no one except Stephens. It was a divorce care class. What? Lord, I thought You showed me I was healed from my divorce. I have been divorced for five years. You took me through the rigors of forgiving my ex-husband. I have cried and cried and prayed and prayed. Why am I here? What have I missed? What crevice still needs Your soothing touch? I so desire to be whole, to be healed.

Class proceeded with discussions and a video. Throughout the video I was pleading with God to reveal to me what I need to learn. In what area of my life have I not healed? Please, please, please show me, Father. I beg of You…help me understand.

After the video, Stephens announced to the class, "I guess you are all wondering why I have invited Stella here tonight." Meanwhile, in my head, I am wondering why he invited Stella to this gathering.

The next statement out of Stephens' mouth almost made me fall out of my chair. "Stella is the picture of HOPE because she has chosen to make God her center of gravity". That's why I'm here? God is showing me I AM healed!!!

Yeah!!! I have not been way off base. I have understood God!! Yippee!!!

Thank You LORD for healing me! Thank You for saving my soul! Thank You LORD for understanding my needs and bringing me through the mire to a better place.

If you find yourself in an uncertain place, a space of confusion, I encourage you to absorb yourself in God's Word and fall before Him in prayer asking for guidance and healing.

I hope the following verses will be of benefit to you on your journey.

2 Kings 20:5
Thus says the LORD, the God of David your father; I have heard your prayer; I have seen your tears. Behold, I will heal you.

Jeremiah 17:14
Heal me, O LORD, and I shall be healed; save me, and I shall be saved, for you are my praise.

Jeremiah 30:17
For I will restore health to you, and your wounds I will heal, declares the LORD

Isaiah 38:17
Behold, it was for my welfare that I had great bitterness; but in love you have delivered my life from the pit of destruction, for you have cast all my sins behind your back

Psalm 107:20-21
He sent out his word and healed them, and delivered them from their destruction. Let them thank the LORD for his steadfast love, for his wondrous works to the children of man!

Psalm 30:2
O LORD my God, I cried to you for help, and you have healed me.

Psalm 147:3

He heals the brokenhearted and binds up their wounds.

Matthew 12:20

A bruised reed He will not break,
And smoking flax He will not quench,
Till He sends forth justice to victory

REST AT THE FEET
OF JESUS

Philippians 4: 4-9 (NKJV)
Rejoice in the Lord always. Again I will say, rejoice!

Let your gentleness be known to all men. The Lord is at hand.

Be anxious for nothing, but in everything by prayer and supplication, with thanksgiving, let your requests be made known to God;

and the peace of God which surpasses all understanding, will guard your hearts and minds through Christ Jesus.

Finally, brethren, whatever things are true, whatever things are noble, whatever things are just, whatever things are pure, whatever things are lovely, whatever things are of good report, if there is any virtue and if there is anything praiseworthy—meditate on these things.

The things which you learned and received and heard and saw in me, these do, and the God of peace will be with you.

For years I had been involved in ladies Bible study at our church, and for five years I had served as the facilitator. Through the years I had grown to know Jesus in many roles. He had provided food when I could not see a way to feed my children and I did not have sufficient funds to buy more. I would survey the cabinets and refrigerator and fall to my knees in despondency. I would cry out to Jesus to help me feed my children, help me have enough to prepare breakfast and pack lunches for school. And Lord, please send money. I do not get another paycheck until next week. I was the one with consistent income, Andy was self-employed. My children never knew times were so desperate. The Lord was our Provider.

One night most of the kids were spending the night away. Andy was quite angry with me because I had made clear my intent to leave him and follow through with divorce. I was not in a mood to argue, but he was. He started ramping up and escalating. He was known for his violent tendencies. God showered down an abundance of grace and peace flowed through my veins as the evening intensified.

Andy broke into a fit of rage as we talked in our bedroom. In a matter of minutes, he managed to rip the ceiling fan out of the ceiling, overturn the TV entertainment center and rip our bedroom door off the hinges because he could not control me or convince me to stay. I can proclaim with TOTAL accuracy and confidence I experienced the peace that passes all understanding in the throughs of chaos. My pulse did not go up, and I felt zero fear. God protected me completely from being harmed and becalmed my emotions.

Jesus held my hand as the storm raged around me. It was as if I had a protective shield erected around me. The only words God allowed me to utter in a calm, quiet voice were, "and you wonder why I want to leave." The Lord was my Protector.

This was not Andy's first fit of rage. He had punched holes in the walls, thrown the grill off the deck, overturned bookshelves, broken dishes and much more. I hate to think of the fractures in my children's brains from this environment. My oldest daughter Amy has become a counselor and reassures me that by the grace of God each of my children will be okay. The Lord is our Healer.

To rest at the feet of Jesus makes way for Him to reassure us, to remind of His love and tenderness, kindness and grace. The longer you linger, the more intimate this time becomes. Before you know it, Jesus is your Friend.

My hope through recalling the tough times of my life is that you will see a glimmer of hope and reach out to Jesus for your needs. He will supply all your needs—for He is Provider, Protector, Healer and Friend. Spend time with Him and get to know Him as I have.

Please listen to the song, "Sitting at the Feet of Jesus" written by Ernie Haase and the Gaither Vocal Band, performed by Stephen Curtis Chapman.

WHAT DID I LEARN

Andy and I struggled to communicate effectively. I would say what I felt and he didn't get it or told me I should have different emotions. September 2009, I informed Andy I wanted a divorce. Over the next several months, we worked on logistics. About 3 weeks before I moved out Andy and I found ourselves sitting in our master bathroom, side-by-side on the step which marked the opening of our walk-in shower. For the first time in nearly three decades of trying to communicate, we had the most cohesive, healthy, objective conversation.

Andy: "Do you regret marrying me?"

Stella: "No because I don't regret the children. If I had been married to anyone else, I wouldn't have these children. I never regret the kids…never."

I could have stopped with this comment, but there was more. Andy and I fought viciously and frequently, money was tight, our house was chaos, we lacked cohesiveness and understanding of one another. No matter how the money flowed, we struggled to make ends meet. We lacked a prayer life together and we were mainly at odds with one another.

So, I continued, "if our marriage had been a wonderful, fulfilling relationship, I would not have learned to depend on the Lord the way I have."

Are you listening? Are you paying attention?

I was unable to depend on Andy in numerous ways. I learned to pray more fervently and desperately for my needs. I asked Jesus to provide when my wages were not enough, and Andy had nothing to offer. When I felt alone and needed a hug, but Andy was furious with me and unable to offer affection, I asked Jesus to wrap His arms around me and comfort me. Andy shirked responsibility, but someone in our household of eight had to make decisions and accept responsibility for the functionality of our home and family. I became the default switch, then everything could be blamed on me. Our relationship was far from healthy or fulfilling. Looking back, only by the grace of God we lasted as long as we did.

When the house did not get repaired and I had no money to hire a contractor, without Andy's help, I would cling to John 14: 1-6. When we remodeled, Andy refused to place trim around all four sides of one of our bedroom windows. Three sides were framed for months and months no matter how I asked or pleaded for completion. I hung up a curtain to cover the unfinished frame and clung to John 14: 1-6

John 14:1-6 (NKJV)
The Way, the Truth, and the Life

14 "Let not your heart be troubled; you believe in God, believe also in Me. 2 In My Father's house are many [a] mansions; if *it were* not *so,* [b]I would have told you. I go to prepare a place for you. 3 And if I go and prepare a place for you, I will come again and receive you to Myself; that where I am, *there* you may be also. 4 And where I go you know, and the way you know."

5 Thomas said to Him, "Lord, we do not know where You are going, and how can we know the way?"

6 Jesus said to him, "I am the way, the truth, and the life. No one comes to the Father except through Me.

I am a daughter of the One True King and He has a mansion for me. When the time is perfect, He will call me home to dwell with Him. Shout Hallelujah!!! The mansion for me in my Father's house will have no chaos, no unfinished business, and no emotional duress.

When I was distraught and nine months pregnant with my third child, I really needed to be consoled. Andy was so angry with me that an embrace was totally out of the question. I was extremely great with child (I am five foot one inches tall and stuck out like a large basketball) and the sleep I managed to get was resting in whatever position in the overstuffed chair in the living room. That night I prayed and cried, cried, and prayed. I poured my pitiful little heart out before the Lord. The ugly kind of crying one can do. I petitioned, asking for an embrace…a supernatural embrace. That night it was as if Jesus bent down and wrapped His arms around me in total and unconditional love. That night was the BEST night's sleep I experienced during my entire pregnancy.

> 2 Corinthians 1:4 (NKJV)
> Who comforts us in all our tribulation, that we may be able to comfort those who are in any trouble, with the comfort with which we ourselves are comforted by God.

Throughout my tumultuous and less than enjoyable marriage, I learned to depend on Jesus. I trusted Him for provision, comfort, and strength. I trusted Him for wisdom, courage, and perseverance. God is faithful. Isaiah 61: 1 tells us "The Spirit of the Lord God is upon me, because the Lord has anointed me to bring good news to the poor; he has sent me to bind up the brokenhearted, to proclaim liberty to the captives, and the opening of the prison to those who are bound."

My heart has HOPE in the Lord, because I have been released from bondage!

PRAISE YOU IN
THE STORM

Good morning! Each moment of every day we have something to be thankful for. We have much to be thankful for. As I pen this, the wind howls outside my windows and screeches to cause destruction or push through the coming cold front.

We were awakened this morning around 4:30am by a loud KABOOM, it sounded as if a bomb was exploding. The sound was so tremendously loud, as if the entire house was caving in. The house shook and I woke in shock. Not sure why, but the words that erupted out of my mouth were, "it is a catastrophe"!!! Tuck was waking up from a sound sleep and did not understand my cause for alarm.

When I rushed to the living room, there was debris all over the floor; but I could not determine what type of debris I was observing. I have seen videos of curious cats climbing and toppling over Christmas trees. Oh, did I mention, it is December 23rd (my oldest son Jake's birthday)? My tree was intact, with lights and decorations unfettered. Then Tuck looks up, the ceiling is not intact. There are two gaping holes in the ceiling. The debris is sheetrock. I hope everyone enjoys a little bit of dust in their gift bag.

We stepped out onto the deck where tree branches covered the deck—this was a new development. There in the chilly 22 degrees and the eeriness of the moonlit night sky we could see something more. Tuck said repeatedly, "oh no, oh no" as we witnessed a giant tree resting on the corner of my home after it had made a prejudice intrusion at the corner of the house. Tuck took my hand and guided me down the hallway toward my bedroom.

My dear elderly mother (96 years young) called from the sitting room portion of my bedroom for us to assess the damage near her. As we enter my bedroom, shock is barely the word to describe the feeling piercing through my chest. A large tree branch was protruding through the ceiling into the middle of my room. The branch had entered the trey ceiling just above where my bed was usually positioned. Had I been sleeping in my bed, all the rubble from the storm damage would have landed on my head. I certainly would have been killed or critically injured. And my precious Mama, was sleeping 15 feet from where this intruder thrust itself into our living space. How could I forgive myself if something had happened to her?

In August, God urged me to place my house on the market. With this decision, I purged many things out of my home, gave away furniture and put other items in storage. I gave my mattress to my youngest daughter at college and disassembled the frame to the garage. This night I was sleeping in my daughter's room, and my life was spared.

Praise God for these circumstances. Had my home not been up for sale, I would have been sleeping just below where the branch invaded my bedroom. Examining the debris of shingles and rafters on my floor made me realize how God protected me in this event. And this week of the year traditionally my daughter Amy and her daughter Grace sleep in my bed with me. Due to work schedules of my adult children, we scheduled Christmas late. A few days ago, I had a conversation with my prayer warrior friend Matt who relayed to me how he has been taught through life's trials to be thankful in ALL circumstances.

Rattled with tons of adrenaline coursing through my veins, I was so hot I did not detect the rush of cold air cascading through my roof into the bedroom. Tuck safely moved my mom to Lizzy's room. My mom was filled with the peace that passes all understanding, she was able to comfortably crawl in bed, cover up and relax to sleep a little longer within 30 minutes of our sleep disruption. I was in a stir for three hours. When I did fall asleep for about an hour, I dreamed of nothing but horror surrounding the damage to my home. Curious how our minds try to make sense of it all.

As Tuck and I sat at the dining room table, pondering the night, he played "Praise You in the Storm". Please take time to listen.

Lord, help me see the blessings in the middle of my house having catastrophic damage. My eyes are darting, my thoughts are racing, my heart is pounding, and I could cry at any moment. Ever been overwhelmed to this extent? Maybe it was not damage to your home or maybe it was a trusted relationship that went catastrophically in the wrong direction. Does this damage delay me moving forward, going to a new chapter? My thoughts are so scattered I wrestle to gather them…Help me, Lord.

I moved Mama and me to a hotel room in town, Tuck said he was okay for now to stay at the house with the dogs. The events that followed are comical to think of looking back, but not too funny at the time. Being so exhausted in the afternoon, I laid down in the hotel room for 20 minutes of rest when the fire alarm went off. We were on the second floor, my Mom has a walker and cannot mobilize quickly. How can I get her safely out of the room and to the car? We managed. The poor receptionist at the desk was frantically attempting to turn off the alarm as we entered the lobby. The extreme cold (9 degrees in Georgia) had gotten the automatic doors confused, set off the alarm and sprinkler system at the front door of the hotel. The atrium between the two sets of doors looked like a rain forest with its cascade of water flowing down. Due to the cold, the flowing water quickly turned to ice in the parking lot. What a mess, we moved from one catastrophe to another. My emotions were shot. I was past numb.

I spoke with insurance agents and adjusters that day. The very kind adjuster and his wife reassured me that due to the significance of the damage, he would be at my house on Monday, but normally they would not have an appointment for a month. God was taking care of me, but I had trouble seeing it.

Sunday morning, Christmas Day 2022, as I sat in the tub at the hotel, weeping in my overwhelmed state, I took my avalanche of emotions to my Heavenly Father. I was a puddle of tears in a puddle of warm water. As I wept, He reassured me that He did not allow Satan to harm me personally. He reminded me of Job, who lost everything, but God did not allow Satan to take Job's life. I knew God had a purpose in the devastating blow to my home and in time, I would see His provision and wisdom.

We went to church Sunday morning. What a nice Christmas message, during which the teaching pastor asked, "Can you think of a time in your life God spared your life? He spared you from something because of His grace and mercy." I was a mess, a broken, sobbing, and overwhelmed mess. I knew that I knew that I knew God had shown His mercy to ME and spared my life. Recall a time you know God has been merciful in your life—sit there and dwell in that space.

Have you noticed the correlation between serving and obeying God and how Satan tries to shred you the closer you get to God? My house was destroyed, approximately $100K worth of damage, at 4:30 am on December 23, 2022. I signed with a publisher and paid my deposit for this book around 2 pm on December 22, 2022. To God be the GLORY!!

Psalm 25:10 (NKJV)
All the paths of the LORD *are* mercy and truth,
To such as keep His covenant and His testimonies.

Deuteronomy 7:9 NKJV)
"Therefore, know that the LORD your God, He *is* God, the faithful God who keeps covenant and mercy for a thousand generations with those who love Him and keep His commandments"

Isaiah 30:18 (NKJV)
Therefore, the LORD will wait, that He may be gracious to you;
And therefore He will be exalted, that He may have mercy on you.
For the LORD *is* a God of justice;
Blessed *are* all those who wait for Him.

Lamentations 3:22-23 (NKJV)
Through the LORD's mercies we are not consumed,
Because His compassions fail not.
They are new every morning;
Great is Your faithfulness.

Titus 3:5 (NKJV)
not by works of righteousness which we have done, but according to His mercy He saved us, through the washing of regeneration and renewing of the Holy Spirit

A Heavenly Inheritance
1 Peter 1: 3-9 (NKJV)

[3] Blessed *be* the God and Father of our Lord Jesus Christ, who according to His abundant mercy has begotten us again to a living hope through the resurrection of Jesus Christ from the dead, [4] to an inheritance [b]incorruptible and undefiled and that does not fade away, reserved in heaven for you, [5] who are kept by the power of God through faith for salvation ready to be revealed in the last time.

[6] In this you greatly rejoice, though now for a little while, if need be, you have been [c]grieved by various trials, [7] that the genuineness of your faith, *being* much more precious than gold that perishes, though it is tested by fire, may be found to praise, honor, and glory at the revelation of Jesus Christ, [8] whom having not [d]seen you love. Though now you do not see *Him,* yet believing, you rejoice with joy inexpressible and full of glory, [9] receiving the end of your faith—the salvation of *your* souls.

EZEKIEL 47

In the pit of my despair, God has my lifetime friend send a text, "Stella, Ezekiel 47, read it. It is for you!" My friend has no idea what I have been dealing with, but God does. May this passage serve as encouragement to you.

Ezekiel 47 (NKJV)
The Healing Waters and Trees

47 Then he brought me back to the door of the [a]temple; and there was water, flowing from under the threshold of the temple toward the east, for the front of the temple faced east; the water was flowing from under the right side of the temple, south of the altar. ² He brought me out by way of the north gate, and led me around on the outside to the outer gateway that faces east; and there was water, running out on the right side.

³ And when the man went out to the east with the line in his hand, he measured one thousand cubits, and he brought me through the waters; the water *came up to my* ankles. ⁴ Again he measured one thousand and brought me through the waters; the water *came up to my* knees. Again he measured one thousand and brought me through; the water *came up to my* waist. ⁵ Again he measured one thousand, *and it was* a river that I could not cross; for the water was too deep, water in which one must swim, a river that could not be crossed. ⁶ He said to me, "Son of man,

have you seen *this?*" Then he brought me and returned me to the bank of the river.

⁷ When I returned, there, along the bank of the river, *were* very many trees on one side and the other. ⁸ Then he said to me: "This water flows toward the eastern region, goes down into the [b]valley, and enters the sea. *When it* reaches the sea, *its* waters are healed. ⁹ And it shall be *that* every living thing that moves, wherever [c]the rivers go, will live. There will be a very great multitude of fish, because these waters go there; for they will be healed, and everything will live wherever the river goes. ¹⁰ It shall be *that* fishermen will stand by it from En Gedi to En Eglaim; they will be *places* for spreading their nets. Their fish will be of the same kinds as the fish of the Great Sea, exceedingly many. ¹¹ But its swamps and marshes will not be healed; they will be given over to salt. ¹² Along the bank of the river, on this side and that, will grow all *kinds of* trees used for food; their leaves will not wither, and their fruit will not fail. They will bear fruit every month, because their water flows from the sanctuary. Their fruit will be for food, and their leaves for medicine."[d]

Borders of the Land

¹³ Thus says the Lord GOD: "These *are* the borders by which you shall divide the land as an inheritance among the twelve tribes of Israel. Joseph *shall have two* portions. ¹⁴ You shall inherit it equally with one another; for I raised My hand in an oath to give it to your fathers, and this land shall fall to you as your inheritance.

¹⁵ "This *shall be* the border of the land on the north: from the Great Sea, *by* the road to Hethlon, as one goes to Zedad, ¹⁶ Hamath, Berothah, Sibraim (which *is* between the border of Damascus and the border of Hamath), to

Hazar Hatticon (which *is* on the border of Hauran). [17] Thus the boundary shall be from the Sea to Hazar Enan, the border of Damascus; and as for the north, northward, it is the border of Hamath. *This is* the north side.

[18] "On the east side you shall mark out the border from between Hauran and Damascus, and between Gilead and the land of Israel, along the Jordan, and along the eastern side of the sea. *This is* the east side.

[19] "The south side, toward the [e]South, *shall be* from Tamar to the waters of [f]Meribah by Kadesh, along the brook to the Great Sea. *This is* the south side, toward the South.

[20] "The west side *shall be* the Great Sea, from the *southern* boundary until one comes to a point opposite Hamath. This *is* the west side.

[21] "Thus you shall divide this land among yourselves according to the tribes of Israel. [22] It shall be that you will divide it by lot as an inheritance for yourselves, and for the strangers who dwell among you and who bear children among you. They shall be to you as native-born among the children of Israel; they shall have an inheritance with you among the tribes of Israel. [23] And it shall be *that* in whatever tribe the stranger dwells, there you shall give *him* his inheritance," says the Lord GOD.

May this serve as encouragement to you, that you are exactly where God would have you be. He loves you and orchestrates your steps. He wants you to look forward in HOPE at the future He has planned for you.

LOOK UP CHILD

Father, I fall before You in total discouragement. I know, logically, I have MANY things to be thankful for. I am thankful. I am very thankful, but I am also very human…and discouraged.

Help me Father, help me to trust You. Help me to remember ALL the good You have done in my life. Help me to remember when I felt overwhelmed and engulfed by my circumstances, You have always made a way.

As a Christian, I know I am to be hopeful…but recently it has been tough. I don't like it when I feel low. I know, once again, logically, and spiritually, I should be hopeful and hold my head high because I am a daughter of the ONE true King. But day after day…I wait. I wait to hear about my house and when the restoration can start. I wait to hear from my Sweetie as to when our way forward together can start. I wait and wait and wait. I work and work and work. I've worked full time and over time since I was 14 years old. I am not lazy, and I do not mind working. I struggle to see light at the end of the tunnel.

My dear friend Troy encourages me. He says, "Stella, you know God has never left you and He has never forsaken you. He has carried you through tough times that should have killed you. It's a miracle you have come this far". Troy is right. God has been faithful and delivered me from much. He has saved me from tremendous circumstances of which I have no knowledge. God loves me…so why do I fall into discouragement? God blatantly spared my life the night the tree fell on the roof and cascaded into my bedroom. Had my home not been for sale, I would have been sleeping directly under where the debris and tree crashed through the roof. I could have been killed or seriously injured.

I am desperate to move forward, what else Father? What else? Why can't I go forward? Then at work, we have a patient who is in her last days…as I have the difficult but necessary conversation with the sister who is having trouble letting go. The sister touches my arm, holds my hand and with crocodile tears in her eyes says, "God sent you to us". How can I feel so discouraged when I am obviously where God wants me to be? And He is using me to touch others for Him.

This morning, I woke up in an overwhelming sea of discouragement. It has been over two months since the tree struck my house, and no repairs have started. Emergently, the 80' tree was removed in frigid temperatures on Christmas Eve. Weathering boards and tarps were placed to secure the home. Otherwise, nothing has moved forward. We waited for more than a month for the structural engineer to evaluate. Then we waited for 15 more days for the engineer's report—21 linear feet of structural damage. This repair is necessary before we can think about sheet rock, paint, or flooring.

The adjuster could do no line-item review or reconciliation prior to the assessment of the engineer. Now I find out, on Saturday, while I am wrestling with a heavy workload and cold symptoms, that the adjuster I trust has been taken off my claim. There is so much damage that it led to large claims loss. Why? To speed up repairs. Are we serious right now? Oh, my adjuster had been removed from my claim about 7-10 days before… and no one informed me. Lord, I am human and not a super one of those at present. I am croaking, really croaking.

I am thankful to not be in my home each day or I believe full depression would have set in by now. I am working in the Northern Tundra on contract, but my son Tuck is living in the house. The house that has been in limbo for nearly three months, holes in the roof, tarp on top and debris in various rooms.

Sometimes I feel like a toddler, throwing myself on the floor in utter frustration because I lack the ability to change my situation. I am kicking and screaming out of irritation and resentment, and at the same time "tryusting" to trust God and His timing. I apologize to the Almighty for lacking trust in this situation and lacking the patience just to wait out the process.

Other days I feel like a perpetual four-year-old. Why? Why, Father, do I have to go through this right now? Why do I have to wait? Why can't I move forward? Why can't my Sweetie be by my side as I go through these challenges? Why do I have speed bump after speed bump when I am trying to serve You and live my life correctly according to Your statutes?

Am I the only one who gets this frustrated and undone? I am so discouraged. Lately, I feel like I am wallowing around in a puddle of discouragement. Some days it is as big as an ocean of discouragement—not self-pity, just discouragement. It is quite a challenge to put a smile on my face and march confidently through the day.

Abba Father,

I am limp in front of You, dejected and emotionally torn. Weary, that is me. Weary from the valleys and little mountain top. Can I have some mountain tops? Just a smidgen would be awesome. When I am sick, it would be delightful to have my Sweetie here—he would care for me. He would fix me a cup of hot tea or a bowl of homemade soup.

Father, I am not asking to win the lottery. You fully recognized when Adam was alone, he was not complete. You made a helpmeet for him when You created Eve. Why do I face these earthly challenges without my other half?

I am helpless about the house. I am powerless. I know I am your daughter, but I fall before You with no strength, no ability to influence and no provisions to make the situation better.

Help me to trust You more. Help me to admit my full dependence on You for each day as we move forward. Help me to trust Your timing. Help me to not get discouraged when I take two steps forward and five steps back.

Help me. Your WORD says in Philippians 4:19 (NKJV) "and my God will supply all your need according to His riches in glory by Christ Jesus". Do you feel I do not need my other half? Why Lord, why?

I will trust TRUTH. You are LOVE, You are FAITHFUL and You work all things together for our GOOD. I cannot stand on how I feel, I must cling to Your WORD—TRUTH.

There is so much I do not understand. I struggle with seeing my circumstances from Your perspective. Help me. Unravel the confusion I face and help me to see Your plan clearly. Help me to know the next step and bring my emotions in line because I am unable.

In the Name of Jesus…Amen

So, how as a Christian, do you have perpetual hope in these circumstances? I know I am not in the same space I was in when I was married to Andy, but having my current house injured is emotionally devastating to me. I have scars from years of lies about a home I loved. My current home is one that God made a way for me to purchase when the world said I did not qualify. How can we get passed this tree injury? In a reasonable amount of time?

Each day that passes without any steps forward my brain processes as "Stella, you are stuck", "you will never move forward". I know this is Satan attacking me but how do I get the attack to stop when no motion has happened in a forward direction. How do I remain unequivocally hopeful in the face of no progress?"

So, being respectful of Almighty God, I still have questions. When is it my turn, Father? How long must I wait? Still, I walk this path alone. I know who my Sweetie is but am not allowed to be with him in a personal way until the junk is cleared out of my own life (I guess, I am not sure what I am waiting on). Feel like I am perpetually held back.

Why is it necessary for me to tread this path without my Sweetie by my side? I know he would be encouraging and uplifting when I slump. Shoot, he would have given me hot tea and a bowl of homemade soup when I returned from work with cold symptoms. I am not asking for a mountain. Why must I face these challenges without my earthly companion? Why?

I look around—couples, couples together, couples getting engaged, couples getting married, couples enjoying companionship together. Even my own daughter, Amy, recently divorced, has a sweetheart who understands her, encourages her and is kind to family. When is it my turn? How long must I wait? It seems like I am waiting for everything.

Lord, have mercy on me. I meet other women who have been through difficult abusive marriages/relationships, and they desire to be with no one. Father, that is not me. Be merciful, Father. Can I please have my soulmate walk hand in hand with me through the house stuff? Of do I have to wait until the house is all put back together? It feels like forever.

Romans 8:28 (NKJV) tells us, "and we know that all things work together for good to them that love God, to them who are the called according to His purpose."

How is this brutal loneliness good? I am crumbling.

As Your child, I know Your answer—Look Up Child. You want me to cry to you first and foremost…not moan and groan to my friends. I fall prostrate before Your throne. Help me to trust when I do not see an end to my loneliness. Help me to trust You are capturing every tear that falls, that my tears are not in vain. Father, I have shed so many. Help me to trust You will hold me, reassure me, comfort me when I feel so alone. Please do not misinterpret this writing, I know God is Holy, Perfect, Love and Kindness, full of Grace. He knows what gifts are correct and His timing is perfect.

In humility and guilt, I fall before Him asking for anything at all. He has sacrificed His Son, so I do not spend eternity in hell and eternal damnation. How can I ask for more? Because I am unbelievably human, through and through.

Take a few minutes to listen to Lauren Daigle's *"Look Up Child"*

What I have come to realize is God IS love, He IS faithful and He desires his children to come to Him for everything. We can go freely to Almighty God for comfort, reassurance, guidance, uplifting, forgiveness, strength, protection, and provision.

My daddy studied at seminary and learned Hebrew and Greek. He would tell me that in Genesis 1:1 God is called Elohim. Elohim in Hebrew means "God the breast". He is ALL sustenance to His children as a mother is all sustenance to a suckling infant. Anyone who has breastfed a baby or been close to a nursing mother knows the infant believes Mama is EVERYTHING. When a baby latches onto the mother's breast to feed, this encounter encompasses so much more. This intimate interaction provides nourishment, comfort, warmth, emotional support, and reassurance simultaneously.

God desires his children come to Him for any problem, any emotion, and any circumstance. He is omniscient and knows where we are and what we are about. Ask Him to help you trust…trust His character, trust His Word and trust that He loves you.

Printed in the USA
CPSIA information can be obtained
at www.ICGtesting.com
LVHW041200131124
795860LV00038B/66